Nayef R.F. Al-Rodhan (ed.)

Policy Briefs on the *Transnational* Aspects of Security and Stability

Policy Briefs on the *Transnational* Aspects of Security and Stability

edited by
Nayef R.F. Al-Rodhan

LIT

Gedruckt auf alterungsbeständigem Werkdruckpapier entsprechend
ANSI Z3948   DIN ISO 9706

Cover picture: First Assembly of the League of Nations, Geneva, 1920

Bibliographic information published by the Deutsche Nationalbibliothek
The Deutsche Nationalbibliothek lists this publication in the Deutsche Nationalbibliografie; detailed bibliographic data are available in the Internet at http://dnb.d-nb.de.

ISBN-10: 3-03735-149-7 (Switzerland)
ISBN-10: 3-8258-0180-2 (Germany)

ISBN-13: 978-3-03735-149-9 (Switzerland)
ISBN-13: 978-3-8258-0180-9 (Germany)

© LIT VERLAG GmbH & Co. KG Wien,
Zweigniederlassung Zürich 2007
Dufourstr. 31
CH-8008 Zürich
Tel. +41 (0) 44-251 75 05
Fax +41 (0) 44-251 75 06
e-Mail: zuerich@lit-verlag.ch
http://www.lit-verlag.ch

LIT VERLAG Dr. W. Hopf
Berlin
Dietrich-Bonhoeffer-Haus
Ziegelstr. 30
D-10177 Berlin

Auslieferung:
Deutschland: LIT Verlag Fresnostr. 2, D-48159 Münster
Tel. +49 (0) 2 51/620 32 - 22, Fax +49 (0) 2 51/922 60 99, e-Mail: vertrieb@lit-verlag.de

Distributed in the UK by: Global Book Marketing, 99B Wallis Rd, London, E9 5LN
Phone: +44 (0) 20 8533 5800 – Fax: +44 (0) 1600 775 663
http://www.centralbooks.co.uk/acatalog/search.html

Distributed in North America by:

Transaction Publishers
New Brunswick (U.S.A.) and London (U.K.)

Transaction Publishers
Rutgers University
35 Berrue Circle
Piscataway, NJ 08854

Phone: +1 (732) 445 - 2280
Fax: + 1 (732) 445 - 3138
for orders (U. S. only):
toll free (888) 999 - 6778
e-mail:
orders@transactionspub.com

CONTENTS

	Acknowledgements	i
	List of Contributors	ii
1	**The Transnational Policy Brief Series** NAYEF R.F. AL-RODHAN	1
2	**Is NATO Going Global?** FRED TANNER	5
3	**Editorial of Policy Brief on Is NATO Going Global?** NAYEF R.F. AL-RODHAN	13
4	**Security in the Caspian Sea Region: Challenges and Opportunities in a Globalized World** EKATERINA SHADRINA	19
5	**Editorial of Policy Brief on Security in the Caspian Sea Region: Challenges and Opportunities in a Globalized World** NAYEF R.F. AL-RODHAN	35
6	**Prevention of WMD Proliferation, Globalization, and International Security** VLADIMIR ORLOV	39
7	**Editorial of Policy Brief on Prevention of WMD Proliferation, Globalization, and International Security** NAYEF R.F. AL-RODHAN	55
8	**The Non-Proliferation Regime** SHAHRAM CHUBIN	61
9	**Editorial of Policy Brief on The Non-Proliferation Regime** NAYEF R.F. AL-RODHAN	69

10	Proliferation, Non-state Actors, and the Impact on Global Security WAHEGURU PAL SINGH SIDHU	75
11	Editorial of Policy Brief on Proliferation, Non-state Actors, and the Impact on Global Security NAYEF R.F. AL-RODHAN	83
12	Arms Control in a Globalized World PÁL DUNAY	89
13	Editorial of Policy Brief on Arms Control in a Globalized World NAYEF R.F. AL-RODHAN	101
14	Energy Security, Globalization, and Global Security JOHN C. GAULT	107
15	Editorial of Policy Brief on Energy Security, Globalization, and Global Security NAYEF R.F. AL-RODHAN	119
16	Water, Globalization, and Global Security PETER H. GLEICK	125
17	Editorial of Policy Brief on Water, Globalization, and Global Security NAYEF R.F. AL-RODHAN	143
18	Natural Disasters, Globalization, and the Implications for Global Security EMILY MUNRO	149
19	Editorial of Policy Brief on Natural Disasters, Globalization, and the Implications for Global Security NAYEF R.F. AL-RODHAN	163
20	Changing Health Paradigms, Globalization, and Global Security BATES GILL XIAOQING LU	169

21	**Editorial of Policy Brief on Changing Health Paradigms, Globalization, and Global Security** NAYEF R.F. AL-RODHAN	179
22	**US Environmental Policy and Global Security** JENNIFER WALLACE	185
23	**Editorial of Policy Brief on US Environmental Policy and Global Security** NAYEF R.F. AL-RODHAN	197
24	**Identifying Transnational Solutions for Our Globalized World** NAYEF R.F. AL-RODHAN	203
	Index	207

Acknowledgements

I would like to take this opportunity to extend my gratitude to those who have assisted me in the publication of this work.

I am grateful to Ambassador Gérard Stoudmann for his wisdom and guidance; Dr. Fred Tanner for his mentoring and his insights; Paul Clark for his research assistance; Bethany Webster for her administrative and drafting assistance.

Thank you also to Lisa Watanabe and Ekaterina Rykovanova for their dedication to our program and for their contributions to this work.

Of course, we are also grateful to all of our authors who have made this work possible through their insightful contributions. The program is also indebted to our editors, Curtis Budden, Jean Callaghan, and Christopher Findlay.

Finally, this publication could not have been possible without the collaboration with the faculty and staff of the Geneva Centre for Security Policy. The program is grateful for their continued support.

NOTES ON THE CONTRIBUTORS

Nayef R.F. Al-Rodhan, M.D., PhD., is Senior Scholar in Geostrategy and the Director of the Program on the Geopolitical Implications of Globalization and Transnational Security at the Geneva Centre for Security Policy, Geneva, Switzerland.

Fred Tanner is Director of the Geneva Centre for Security Policy, Geneva, Switzerland.

Ekaterina Shadrina is Project Officer, Middle East and Russian Federation at the Geneva Centre for Security Policy, Geneva, Switzerland.

Vladimir Orlov is Course Co-Director of the European Training Course in Security Policy at the Geneva Centre for Security Policy, Geneva, Switzerland.

Shahram Chubin is Director of Studies and Joint Course Director of the International Training Course in Security Policy at the Geneva Centre for Security Policy, Geneva, Switzerland.

Waheguru Pal Singh Sidhu is Course Director of the New Issues in Security Course at the Geneva Centre for Security Policy, Geneva, Switzerland.

Pál Dunay is former Director of the International Training Course in Security Policy at the Geneva Centre for Security Policy, Geneva, Switzerland and Senior Researcher at the Stockholm International Peace Research Institute, Stockholm, Sweden.

John C. Gault is President of John Gault SA and Associate Faculty Member at the Geneva Centre for Security Policy, Geneva, Switzerland.

Peter H. Gleick is President of the Pacific Institute, Oakland, California, United States.

Emily Munro is Training and Academic Affairs Coordinator at the Geneva Centre for Security Policy, Geneva, Switzerland.

Bates Gill holds the Freeman Chair in China Studies at the Center for Strategic and International Studies, Washington, DC, United States.

Xiaoqing Lu is Research Associate with the Freeman Chair in China Studies at the Center for Strategic and International Studies, Washington, DC, United States.

Jennifer Wallace is Course Coordinator for the International Training Course in Security Policy at the Geneva Centre for Security Policy, Geneva, Switzerland.

CHAPTER 1

THE TRANSNATIONAL POLICY BRIEF SERIES

NAYEF R.F. AL-RODHAN

Dr. Nayef R.F. Al-Rodhan is Senior Scholar in Geostrategy and Director of the Program on the Geopolitical Implications of Globalization and Transnational Security at the Geneva Centre for Security Policy, Geneva, Switzerland

Introduction

The policy brief series at the Geneva Centre for Security Policy (GCSP) was created by the Program on the Geopolitical Implications of Globalization and Transnational Security in order to analyze the current trends in policy-making and agenda-setting processes within nation-states and to identify the implications for the international system. The program itself is based on thematic as well as policy-based approaches to globalization and security, giving its publications and perspectives a unique position within the academic literature. The policy brief series provides the policy angle to the program's publications. This edition, which focuses on transnational security and stability, looks at the problems that states are faced with, government responses, and the implications of these policies, and contributes precise and tangible policy recommendations for governments.

The authors include a number of academics and individuals whose perspectives represent a variety of backgrounds, and the range of topics they discuss is very diverse. It is important to note that the authors' contributions represent their own viewpoints and not the opinions or policies of the GCSP or its globalization program. Rather, the authors were asked to contribute their own perspectives and expertise. This approach has resulted in a broad range of analysis and a great variety of topics.

Despite the diversity of topics, the briefs share the same basic structure. Each brief discusses one topical area in terms of policy challenges, current responses to the challenges, policy dilemmas created by these responses, implications, and future scenarios, and concludes with policy recommendations that governments should follow in order to promote international security and stability. Within this framework, we found it necessary to add the views of the program to the briefs, and therefore created the editorial sub-series that analyzes the issues from the program's perspective and from my own point of view. With this addition, the Program on the Geopolitical Implications of Globalization and Transnational Security has also contributed to the brief.

The structure of the editorials is simple and allows for further, more concise analysis. The circle provides the reader with an illustrative format to show the linkages between the various challenges and the related recommendations. In addition, the circle provides a visual aid for further discussion of the topic and demonstrates that the dilemmas and recommendations that are presented exert influence beyond their own immediate scope. Rather, each problem, and each related policy recommendation is impacted by parallel developments in other states, particularly when states develop their own national responses. Because of the reciprocal effects of policy challenges and policy recommendations, we have chosen the circle as an appropriate representation of the issues that arise.

Policy Briefs on the Transnational Aspects of Security and Stability
The briefs that make up this volume focus on the structures of the state and its functions and on the specific threats and challenges to these functions. Therefore, this volume discusses topics such as arms control, environmental policy, proliferation of weapons of mass destruction, and water and energy security. The transnational aspects of security and stability often include aspects of national security, and this publication focuses not on the human element of decision making, but rather on those aspects that involve the functioning of the state.

Other topics addressed in this volume include treaties, international law, natural disasters, and regional security structures. The way that states are currently negotiating their role in the international system is a critical factor that will shape the future trends and trajectories in security issues. Globalization is often cited as the reason for the changing role of the state in new security and international structures, and these briefs look at that phenomenon from a number of different angles and using examples from within state structures. The topics discussed – such as states' efforts to interdict proliferation of banned weapons to non-state actors, the reworking of the Nuclear Non-Proliferation Treaty in light of recent events in Iran and North Korea, and the changing role of the North Atlantic Treaty Organisation (NATO) – all relate to the broad subject of reforming state structures.

By assessing the current operations of state structures and ways in which they are changing, we will be able to identify the best ways to improve decision-making and policy-making processes. The broad range of subjects discussed in this volume from the transnational perspective will provide a solid basis for an understanding of some current trends and future agenda setting within the globalization and security debate.

CHAPTER 2

IS NATO GOING GLOBAL?

FRED TANNER

Dr. Fred Tanner is Director of the Geneva Centre for Security Policy, Geneva, Switzerland

Abstract
The major policy challenge for NATO is to find a legitimate and credible role as a security provider in a globalized security environment. Thus, the question arises whether NATO will have to go global in order to remain relevant as an international security institution in the 21st century. NATO is unique in its ability to conduct robust military operations in an interoperable framework that could serve as a global force generator. In order to become a global security provider, NATO has to overcome antagonism with the EU as well as its transatlantic mindset. For this purpose, NATO needs a new strategic concept based on a common vision.

1. Policy Challenges

Why does the North Atlantic Treaty Organisation (NATO) still exist and why did it not disappear with the end of the Cold War? Established as a Western shield against the Soviet bloc at the outset of the Cold War, critics charge that it now struggles to remain relevant. Having transformed itself from a collective defense organization to a collective security agent, NATO currently assumes not only multiple roles, but also multiple identities. The major policy challenge for NATO is to find a legitimate and credible role as a security provider in a globalized security environment where military power is of only limited value. Globalization has made societies more vulnerable to cross-cutting challenges and threats, such as infectious diseases, internal conflicts, terrorism, international organized crime, energy resource scarcity, the proliferation of weapons of mass destruction

(WMD), and migration. NATO has only very limited capabilities to address such challenges and threats.

NATO is unique in its ability to conduct robust military operations in an interoperable framework that can generate multinational coalition forces. In the last years, NATO has also become a champion in developing soft power and military-to-military partnerships with the objectives of assisting member states with transformation and post-conflict countries with the reform of their defense and security sectors.

However, the once privileged position of NATO as a security actor is fading quickly. Nowadays, it has to compete and position itself with regards to the European Union (EU), the Organization for Security and Co-operation in Europe, the G8, the United Nations (UN), and even regional organizations in Africa. For a global role, NATO will need the political empowerment of all its member states (most of which are also EU member states), whose societies will have to accept the significant costs entailed by NATO's structural adjustments and capability improvement.

2. Responses

NATO has begun to work with countries outside the broad Euro-Atlantic area through multilayered military-to-military cooperation programs. Such partnerships consist of different layers, with the Partnership for Peace (PfP) program at its core. These partnerships have been extended to the Mediterranean Dialogue and Istanbul Cooperation Initiative (ICI) countries.[1] The partnerships comprise a large spectrum of cooperative activities that engage partner states in interoperability, security governance, defense reforms, defense education, the fight against small arms and light weapons proliferation as well as a range of other activities in the civil-military domain.

NATO's response to the new global security environment has been greatly accelerating since 9/11. For the first time in its history, in support of and solidarity with the United States (US), the alliance invoked on September 12 its collective defense clause (Article 5 of the Washington Treaty.) As part of this move, NATO also launched the maritime operation "Active Endeavour" in the Mediterranean. On a political level, NATO members and partners agreed to a program of cooperation against terrorism in non-military sectors (Partnership Action Plan Against Terrorism).

After the United States overthrew the Taliban regime in Afghanistan, the UN mandated that NATO contribute to the stabilization of that country. This mission marked the first time that NATO agreed to carry out an operation outside Europe. However, if the mission in Afghanistan fails, NATO as an institution will most likely fail, as well. Over the last two years, the organization expanded the scope of its international operations from crisis management to a variety of additional activities, including assistance in training and defense reforms in Iraq, support for disaster relief operations in Pakistan, and logistical support for African Union peace forces in Sudan.

In general, NATO's response to the US-driven global agenda on democratic governance has been both declaratory and programmatic. NATO reasserted its allegiance to liberal principles at its 2004 Istanbul Summit,[2] where it also adopted a policy promoting democratic governance of the defense sector (Partnership Action Plan on Defense Institution Building).

3. Dilemmas

Geographical dilemmas: The US is pushing NATO to become an organization with global reach, in terms of both missions and troop-contributing countries. The US would accept a continuous commitment to NATO only if it is "able to act wherever our interests are threatened."[3] Some European countries are concerned about overstretch and a US instrumentalization of NATO.

Dilemma of mission scope: There is a profound disagreement on how broad the mission spectrum of a future NATO should be. Some European countries, like France, want to see the alliance confined to the defense and military sectors whereas others, including the US as well as NATO Secretary General Jaap de Hoop Scheffer, also envision a future for the organization in areas such as peacebuilding and even peacemaking. Against this backdrop, it's clear that the upcoming development of NATO is hostage to EU-NATO non-relations. While the EU has taken over NATO's peace missions in the Balkans, there is no division of labor "at global and functional levels."[4]

Partnership dilemmas: The Euro-Atlantic Cooperation Council that governs the PfP is dysfunctional, and PfP work programs are now confined to a handful of countries in the Balkans, the

Caucasus, and Central Asia. Many PfP partners have become NATO members and the European neutrals, with the exception of Switzerland, are now investing instead in the battle group arrangement of the EU.

Transformation Dilemma: NATO is caught in a cycle of "reinvention" and transformation in order to adjust to the new global security environment. This transformation is costly; today's political climate, which favors a strengthening of the European Security and Defence Policy (ESDP), hampers these efforts.

Credibility dilemma: NATO has a strong and credible Cold War history. After the end of the Cold War, however, the Alliance's reputation suffered, due to controversy over the 1999 Kosovo intervention. Moreover, NATO has become increasingly perceived, particularly in the developing world, as a proxy organization of the US.

4. Implications

From a geographical or regional perspective, NATO no longer has a specific focus. The 2004 Istanbul Summit has clearly shown that henceforth, NATO's "out of area" debate is over. The organization's agenda in the war against terrorism has enabled it to take a broader and to some extent a global view of security. With the most recent round of enlargement, the "Eastern border" of the Cold War has all but disappeared. The US has been pushing for NATO to get involved in the Middle East and Africa, both militarily and in terms of partnership building. The US Ambassador to NATO recently called for the creation of a global partnership with "contact countries," such as Australia and Japan.[5] In addition, NATO Secretary General Scheffer supports a "transformation" of NATO that would make it global in scope and possibly even in membership. The Autumn 2006 summit in Riga should prepare the basis for such a transformation.[6]

5. Future Trajectories/Scenarios

Strengthened collective defense: In the event that a clear military threat to (some) NATO states would re-emerge, the alliance's role could again shift to deterrence and war fighting capabilities. Such a scenario could arise if an authoritarian and revanchist Russia posed a particular threat to the Baltic NATO States, or in the event of an escalation of nuclear rivalry in the Middle East.

NATO as a toolbox/service center: Due to a lack of sufficient political empowerment, NATO could develop into a mere service provider for *ad hoc* coalitions, disaster relief, humanitarian action, etc. The former German Minister of Defense argued that such a scenario would be unacceptable to the Europeans: "a NATO which is limited to a 'toolbox' role will not be viable."[7]

NATO as stabilizer and peacekeeper: Building on its track record in Bosnia (SFOR/IFOR), Kosovo (KFOR), and Afghanistan (ISAF), NATO could increasingly become the UN's organization of choice for robust and long-term stabilization missions. NATO can provide planning, force generation and the mission-intensity continuum for operations in complex environments. The new NATO Response Force (NRF) can act as a spearhead for preparing the ground for peace missions. The UN, in turn, can provide legitimacy and the instruments for the peacebuilding phase of a conflict. The support mission in Sudan indicates that the UN's demand for NATO missions will be primarily located in Africa.

NATO as a framework for global partnership building: NATO could furthermore become a framework for soft security partnerships at a global level — a development that might be driven by the rise of Asia and the confrontational power transitions entailed therein.[8] This could include associations with current and future troop contributors, such as Australia, Japan or South Korea to form a global partnership. In view of the upcoming NATO summit in Riga, such a partnership is now being discussed.

Fading into oblivion: The strengthening of the European Security and Defence Policy (ESDP), US unilateralism, an estrangement of US-European relations, and insufficient resource allocations to bankroll NATO's transformation may lead to an ineffective and dysfunctional alliance that could fade away within the next 5-10 years.

6. Policy Recommendations

1. In order to remain relevant as a security institution, NATO has to act globally and it must for this purpose develop the necessary capabilities for force projection and sustainable operations.

2. NATO and its members need to agree on a common vision of how NATO can credibly provide security in a globalized world. Such a new vision would require a new strategic concept.

3. The Europeans have to spend more on defense and agree on the pooling of resources and on the specialization of national forces.

The implementation of this recommendation will jeopardize mass conscript armies in Europe.[9]

4. NATO and the EU have to agree on a division of labor, based on their successful cooperation in the Balkans.

5. The US should politically empower NATO and refrain from using it *à la carte* only.

6. NATO should invest more in its successful soft security partnerships, such as PfP, but now on a global scale.

NATO member states should agree to establish a global soft security arrangement, with membership based on criteria of shared values and contributions.

7. NATO should clearly communicate that its global realm be based on democracy and security governance as core principles for its activities.

8. As the relationship with the UN will be key for NATO's role in the 21st century, the Alliance needs to formalize its ties with the UN and develop those capacities that add value to the world organization's quest for peace and security.

The capacities are rapid deployment of expeditionary forces in conflict areas, rapid logistical support to disaster areas and the support of peace mission through force generation.

Acknowledgements

I would like to thank Céline Furi and Derek Lutterbeck for their kind assistance.

References

[1] The Mediterranean Dialogue countries include Algeria, Morocco, Mauritania, Tunisia, Egypt, Jordan, and Israel. The initial focus of the Istanbul Cooperation Initiative is on Bahrain, Kuwait, Oman, Qatar, Saudi Arabia, and the United Arab Emirates.

[2] "Our Alliance is founded on the principles of democracy, individual liberty, and the rule of law," *The Istanbul Declaration: Our Security in a New Era*, June 28, 2004.

[3] "The National Security Policy of the United States of America," Washington, DC, 2002.

[4] P. Dunay and Z. Lachowski, "Euro-Atlantic Security," *SIPRI Yearbook 2006: Armaments, Disarmament and International Security* (Oxford: Oxford University Press, 2006), p. 12.

[5] Speech delivered by Victoria Nuland at the 2006 Partnership for Peace (PfP) Planning Symposium, Oberammergau, Germany, January 19, 2006.

[6] M. Winter, "Nato erwägt Wandel zum Welt-Bündnis," *Süddeutsche Zeitung*, February 3, 2006.

[7] P. Struck, "The Future of NATO," speech delivered at the 40th Munich Conference on Security Policy, February 7, 2004.

[8] J. Kugler, "The Asian Ascent: Opportunity for Peace or Precondition for War?," *International Studies Perspectives*, Vol. 7, Issue 1, February 2006, pp. 36-42.

[9] E. Rhodes, "The Good, the Bad, and the Righteous: Understanding the Bush Vision of a New NATO Partnership," *Millennium*, Vol. 33, No. 1, 2004, p. 141.

CHAPTER 3

EDITORIAL OF POLICY BRIEF ON IS NATO GOING GLOBAL?

NAYEF R.F. AL-RODHAN

Dr. Nayef R.F. Al-Rodhan is Senior Scholar in Geostrategy and Director of the Program on the Geopolitical Implications of Globalization and Transnational Security at the Geneva Centre for Security Policy, Geneva, Switzerland

1. Review and Critique

The North Atlantic Treaty Organisation (NATO) has faced a formidable number of challenges to its existence since its inception in 1949. In the 1960s, there were fears that the future of the Alliance was at risk when France withdrew from its military structure. Diplomats at NATO, however, could well have argued that later arrangements with France to ensure its military support, if required, demonstrate the strength and flexibility of the Alliance. The end of the bipolar system has once again prompted some observers, such as Christopher Layne, to ask whether the death knell should be sounded for NATO.[1] Yet, despite numerous near death experiences, NATO has always managed to re-invent itself. The institution now faces additional challenges posed by a security environment that is being altered not simply by the end of Cold War, but also by the forces of globalization. In order to maintain a legitimate and credible role within this changing context, NATO will have to respond in a fitting manner.

While military security remains relevant to states, globalization has rendered countries more vulnerable to transnational security threats, including infectious diseases, transnational organized criminality, international terrorism, and environmental degradation. Following the demise of the bipolar system, NATO has managed to transform itself from a purely collective defense actor (albeit with an important residual collective defense role) to a collective security actor. However, it still lacks the appropriate tools with which to address multifarious transnational security issues. One of the challenges that the institution faces is that of finding a legitimate and credible role as a soft security provider in an environment in which military power is not always an appropriate means to respond to crises.

Fred Tanner raises a fundamental question in his policy brief: "[W]ill NATO have to go global in order to remain relevant as an international security institution in the 21st century?"[2] At present, little consensus exists as to the appropriate geographical scope of NATO. While the United States (US) is eager to see NATO attain greater global reach, the institution's European members are concerned about possible overstretch. In addition, some member states are also concerned that NATO risks being perceived as a proxy for the US if it acts on a global scale. Despite lack of agreement on the issue, NATO is now acting much further afield than any one would have imagined when the debate about its *raison d'être* began a decade ago.

Another dilemma identified by Tanner relates to the institution's mission. At present, no consensus exists as to what the correct mission of NATO should be. Some member states would like NATO's scope to remain focused on defense and military issues. Others would like to see the institution play a much broader political role while continuing to engage actively in peacekeeping and even peacemaking. In light of 9/11, calls for NATO to play a leading role in the fight against international terrorism have grown louder; as a result, almost every aspect of NATO is reorganized and how it works today has been affected by increased emphasis on fighting terrorism. How NATO responds to the question about its future scope will be vital to determining its relevance.

Yet, as Tanner points out, one of the major issues NATO must resolve is how to coordinate its efforts with other leading security actors. In particular, he argues that NATO needs to overcome its antipathy with the European Union (EU), as well as its transatlantic mindset, in order to become an effective global security actor. In other words, NATO needs to develop a new strategic concept that is premised on a common vision of the future. While transformation of the alliance may be perceived by some as necessary, many European members may prefer to invest their resources in further developing the EU's European Security and Defence Policy (ESDP). Investing in one is of benefit to the other; if EU members enhance their military forces, these same forces could be used for either NATO or EU missions. Indeed, cooperation with the EU is highly likely, as the EU (like

NATO does within the alliance) plays a growing role in coordinating the efforts and resources of EU member states in responding to transnational threats to security. NATO must successfully achieve a true strategic partnership with the EU, one that EU members as well as NATO members agree would be in their common interest. The trick will be for NATO to do so without duplicating what the EU, as well as other security actors, is doing.[3]

2. Dilemmas and Our Recommendations

Globalization and transnational security threats present both opportunities as well as challenges for NATO. In order for the institution to retain its relevance, as well as its legitimacy and credibility, it needs to address a number of issues related to its mission, geographical scope, and partnerships. We highlight eight dilemmas related to this issue area and eight corresponding recommendations that may help generate appropriate responses.

One of the most significant dilemmas facing NATO today relates to today's quickly changing security environment. As mentioned, many of the security challenges that states are confronted with today are non-military and transnational in nature. While this implies a shift in the scope of NATO, the institution also needs to remain true to its institutional foundations. The North Atlantic Treaty states that an armed attack against one or more of NATO's members either in Europe or North America shall be considered as an attack against all members. We suggest that this article needs to be redefined to take into account the altered nature of many of the contemporary threats to security facing NATO's members. Although NATO uses soft power very impressively at times – witness the success of enlargement and the Partnership for Peace, both of which demonstrate that NATO uses soft power to get states to do what it wants, from democratization to the reform of defense institutions – soft power should also be explicitly included in its mandate (e.g. Prague and Istanbul Summit documents),[4] as many of its activities are likely to increasingly involve post-conflict reconstruction and preventive measures.

NATO's regional focus is largely a thing of the past; the alliance is active in the International Security Assistance Force (ISAF)

in Afghanistan, which has been established to help the Afghan Government to provide a secure environment within which to rebuild the country, for instance. We propose that NATO engage in global operations when necessary, as well as to regularly update its security concepts. Yet, since the US is the primary large member state promoting a more global reach for NATO, the institution risks being perceived as a proxy for the US as it increasingly acts "out of area" in the absence of greater global consensus on this issue. In order to avoid this perception, NATO must show independence from Washington, but also solidarity with the US when warranted. Its members should also live up to the institution's political standards, thereby securing the institution's legitimacy and relevance.[5]

Both issues of scope and geographical reach are made more difficult due to disagreements between Europeans as well as within the Atlantic Alliance, as to how best to respond to "new" security challenges. NATO needs to be able to react to more classical threats, as well as be able to respond to ethnic conflicts and to engage in preventive activities in relation to failing states and transnational threats to security. Consensus about the tools required by NATO, as well as its geographical remit, needs to be achieved. Greater dialogue between member states should be promoted regarding NATO's role in a globalizing world. NATO should also educate other regional powers about its role. Without it, NATO's relevance and legitimacy risks being eroded, and coordination with other security actors will be difficult.

3. Conclusion

Having survived challenges to its existence in the past, NATO is now confronted with a changed security environment, in part, as a result of globalization. The most fundamental challenges are related to the kinds of missions that NATO ought to take on, as well as whether it should increasingly define itself as a global security institution. Given the current lack of consensus among its members on these issues, a concerted effort needs to be made in order to develop agreement amongst NATO members as to its role in a changed world. Our aim has been to set out eight dilemmas or challenges facing the institution and to make recommendations that may contribute to the debate.

References

[1] C. Layne, "Death Knell for NATO? The Bush Administration Confronts the European Security and Defense Policy," *Cato Policy Analysis*, No. 394, 2001.
[2] For the brief in its entirety, please see Chapter 2.
[3] See R.A. Clarke, B.R. McCaffrey, and C.R. Nelson, "NATO's Role in Confronting International Terrorism," Atlantic Council of the United States, June 2004.
[4] For examples from the Prague Summit, see the bulletin on Defense against New Threats at http://www.nato.int/docu/update/2002/11-november/e1121e.htm; for the Istanbul Summit see http://www.nato.int/docu/comm/2004/06-istanbul/home.htm.
[5] See C.A. Wallander, "NATO's Price: Shape Up or Ship Out," *Foreign Affairs*, Vol. 81, No. 6, November/December 2002, pp. 2-8.

CHAPTER 4

SECURITY IN THE CASPIAN SEA REGION:
CHALLENGES AND OPPORTUNITIES IN A GLOBALIZED
WORLD

EKATERINA SHADRINA

Ms. Ekaterina Shadrina is Project Officer, Middle East and Russian Federation at the Geneva Centre for Security Policy, Geneva, Switzerland

Abstract
Almost everything written about the Caspian Sea region has referred to the so-called Great Game, when the world powers vied for political control of the region, as well as for its rich mineral resources. Following the break-up of the Soviet Union, the Caspian Sea region was quickly internationalized, emerging as a distinct geopolitical unit and the object of a policy battle on a regional and even global scale. It has recently been an arena for competition among actors both within and outside the region, not only for profits from the development and transportation of Caspian mineral resources but also for influence in the Caucasus and Central Asia.[1] The region's vast hydrocarbon resources make it one of the most promising energy sources for a number of key players: China, the European Union, India, Turkey, and the United States. Nevertheless, despite the potential for long-term economic prosperity, the Caspian region remains one of the world's most complicated geopolitical areas, and one that is very vulnerable to emerging security threats. The Caspian Sea region faces tremendous challenges, including terrorism, unresolved regional conflicts, drug trafficking, proliferation of weapons of mass destruction, environmental degradation, and a lack of regional cooperation. This policy brief examines the key threats that could undermine the region's fragile stability in the immediate future. Its author argues that enhanced regional cooperation and integration among the littoral states are the only means to a possible long-term solution for security in the Caspian Sea region.[2]

1. Policy Challenges

(a) Terrorism, Drug Trafficking, and Weapons of Mass Destruction (WMD) Proliferation
All of the Caspian states see terrorism as a key foreign and domestic threat. It is an especially acute problem for Russia both in terms of the ongoing conflict in Chechnya and because terrorism can spread instability throughout the North Caucasus region, including to the Republic of Dagestan, which is on the Caspian Sea.[3] Terrorism can have a dramatic effect on the security situation in the region due to the possible spread of insurgencies and due to possible attacks on the oil and gas pipelines that are vital to the region's economic development.

A second destabilizing factor in the region is the substantial increase of drug trafficking from Afghanistan. The *2006 International Narcotics Control Strategy Report* released by the United States (US) State Department highlights that all Caspian states continue to serve as major transit countries for drugs originating from Afghanistan.[4]

A third factor threatening stability around the Caspian is the proliferation of weapons of mass destruction. The challenge of preventing WMD proliferation in the region is inevitably interlinked with increasing tensions over Iran's nuclear program, the outcome of which could result in drastic changes for the region's stability. Although the international community is trying to deal with this problem via diplomatic means, a possible US military strike on Iran cannot be ruled out, especially considering that the Bush administration has said that all options are still on the table.[5]

(b) Ensuring Energy Security in the Caspian
It is no secret that the region's oil and gas resources were largely overestimated following the oil boom of the early 1990s. Current oil and gas reserves in the region have been confirmed to be 3-4 percent of the world's known reserves.

There have been both successes and failures in terms of oil and gas exploration in the region, including with respect to the construction of pipelines. This is a competitive environment that is driven by both commercial and political factors. Securing an unbroken energy supply to world markets and diversifying transportation routes have been named priorities by the littoral states, major companies operating in the area, and major external players (China, the European Union (EU), India, Turkey, and the United States).[6] The issue of supply will become even more urgent this year if the prediction that world demand will increase to 1.5 million barrels per day (bpd) from 1.2 million bpd in 2005 comes true. The growth in demand is expected to continue into 2007, when it could reach around 1.8 million bpd.[7]

As a result of a number of large projects, it is predicted that oil production in the region will increase to 400,000 bpd in 2007.[8] It has not been easy, however, to develop the pipeline infrastructure in the region for a number of reasons: the fact that the region is landlocked; the unresolved legal status of the Caspian; the continuing geopolitical rivalry over potential pipeline routes; and the further aggravation of the situation as a result of bureaucracy, corruption, political instability, and regional conflicts. All these factors serve as the main impediments to large-scale investment in the region and to construction of diversified transportation routes that would be highly beneficial for all actors involved.[9]

(c) Environmental Security
There are currently a number of serious threats to environmental security in the region. One of these is so-called bio-terrorism: in this case, the catastrophic depletion of fish stocks as a result of both legal and illegal fishing.[10] Although the oil and gas resources of the region have been widely discussed, the real "black gold" of the Caspian has historically been caviar production, which relies on now endangered sturgeon stocks (more than 85 percent of the world's sturgeon stocks live in the Caspian basin). Experts estimate that the sturgeon population has dropped by 90 percent in the last 30 years (Table 1). Enormous economic losses have resulted from this depletion and the temporary ban on caviar exports imposed by the Convention on International Trade in Endangered Species of Wild Fauna and Flora (the legal caviar trade is estimated at $100 million annually, and much more is thought to be traded on the black market).[11]

2. Responses

(a) Terrorism, Drug Trafficking, and WMD Proliferation
Since 9/11, all Caspian states have tightened security measures in response to the threat of terrorism. The US State Department's *Country Reports on Terrorism* for 2004 reflects the major successes of the littoral states (excluding Iran, naturally) in countering terrorism, including the adoption and ratification of related legal documents, the

prosecution of suspects, the establishment of counterterrorism centers/initiatives, the conduct of law enforcement operations, and an increase in training programs.[12] After a series of deadly attacks in 2004, including explosions in the Moscow metro, two simultaneous suicide attacks targeting commercial airplanes, and the bloody siege of a school in Beslan, Russia tightened security in Chechnya and managed to prevent a major terrorist attack in 2005. Moreover, in 2004-2005, all Caspian states participated in anti-terrorism exercises within the framework of various organizations.[13]

There has been increased cooperation among the littoral states in intercepting narcotics transported across the Caspian Sea by ferry and through border crossings.[14] The decision of all the Central Asian states, Russia, and Azerbaijan to establish a Central Asia Regional Information and Coordination Centre in Almaty, Kazakhstan, which is supported by the United Nations Office on Drugs and Crime (UNODC), is an important step forward in combating drug trafficking. The center will compile and analyze intelligence on drug trafficking and coordinate regional law enforcement operations. Iran's involvement in this initiative could be beneficial since it is a key transit country and the main destination country for Afghan drugs.[15]

The US has been conducting a variety of programs to assist the littoral states (except Iran) in combating the threats of terrorism and drug trafficking, including the Second Line of Defense program and its Megaports Initiative and the Caspian Sea Maritime Interdiction.[16] In addition, the US Department of Defense has allocated more than $135 million for the newly established Caspian Guard program targeting Azerbaijan and Kazakhstan. This program is aimed at assisting these two countries in improving their ability to respond to transnational challenges by providing military consultancy and properly equipping the countries' armed forces. Kazakhstan is part of the US Central Command's area of responsibility, while the US European Command is responsible for operations in Azerbaijan.[17] Russia has also proposed the creation of CASFOR (similar to the Black Sea Task Force) as a "real-time interaction naval group" to fight terrorism, WMD proliferation, organized crime, and also to protect oil and gas infrastructure.[18] It is unlikely to be developed in practice, however, due to the conflicting threat perceptions and security arrangements of the littoral states.

US moves to increase its military presence, including the construction of two radar stations in Azerbaijan (near Iran's northern border and near southern Russia) make both Moscow and Tehran nervous. The Russian and Iranian reactions to the construction were immediate, consistent, and rather predictable, stressing once again their disapproval of the military presence of any third country in the Caspian. Rather, Russia and Iran would prefer to rely on the littoral states to tackle problems and threats. During the meeting in March of the Caspian Working Group in Moscow, Russian Foreign Minister Sergey Lavrov stressed that the littoral states would lose a great deal if they allowed a foreign military presence in the Caspian. While inviting foreign military into the region is not a difficult task, experience has shown that it is much more difficult to get them to leave.[19] Iran elaborated on this point, directly accusing the US of creating obstacles to the development of regional cooperation and regional security arrangements.[20]

At present, no one is calling for the demilitarization of the Caspian Sea region. As Minister Lavrov explained recently: "As to demilitarizing the sea, however attractive this term may sound, it hardly corresponds to the present day realities. In practice such demilitarization would mean disarmament in the Caspian in face of new challenges and threats. On the other hand, the littoral states are not interested in arms buildup in the Caspian, since not a single one of them poses a military threat to each other. Therefore we have suggested that the Convention should embody a formula whereby a stable arms balance of the sides would be maintained, as also [sic] military building within the framework of reasonable sufficiency. It appears to us that this formula is acceptable to all."[21]

Although "not a single one of them poses a military threat to each other," the Caspian states do not seem to consider diplomacy as the only means of solving problems.[22] While there has not yet been a major security incident, states have attempted to protect what they see as their interests (for example, rights to the mineral deposits in the seabed in disputed areas) by threatening the use of force.[23] It is also doubtful that only diplomatic means will be used if Western economic interests (with investments in the region worth billions) are threatened. The Deputy EUCOM (US European Command) Commander stated that the area around the Caspian Sea should be of keen interest to Europeans and that NATO should establish a mission to ensure the safe flow of oil from that region.[24]

Terrorist threats in the Caspian Sea region resulted in increased military budget expenditures in the Caspian states and a quick build-up of their military presence in the region, including the arming of Russia's Caspian Fleet (Table 2). The militarization of the Caspian Sea is a recent, dangerous trend that that makes it clear that the possibility of resorting to military force will not be ruled out in case cooperation and diplomacy fail.

(b) Ensuring Energy Security in the Caspian
There is a possibility that oil and gas production in the region will steadily increase despite a variety of obstacles to the large-scale development of resources. In the long term, most Caspian projects will be Asia-related (China, in particular). China's unprecedented demand for Caspian energy resources has resulted in the investment of billions of dollars in new projects and in the development of regional transport infrastructure. This has made China one of the key external players in the region, while the US role also remains vital. Seeing China's success and efficiency in gaining access to regional resources and contracts for the most attractive projects, India suggested uniting efforts with China in bidding for global energy assets. This includes the Caspian region since it is one of the key areas for both states.[25] At the moment, China is pursuing various projects with all of the Caspian states and is planning to expand its visibility in the region beyond only energy projects. A recently constructed pipeline exporting Kazakh oil to China (with an initial annual capacity of 10 million barrels that will be doubled by 2011 following the extension of the pipeline) has resulted in a shift in the target of oil and gas from the Caspian region." Until recently, the main customers of Caspian energy resources had been in both the European and Mediterranean markets, but now it seems that the Caspian states view the growing Asian market as a priority. Russian Industry and Energy Minister Viktor Khristenko has made it clear that Russia wants to significantly increase oil and gas exports to the Asia-Pacific region, where there is growing demand, especially in light of the desire of Western countries to regulate or reduce energy consumption.[26]

This development poses a serious challenge for Europe, whose dependency on the import of fossil fuels continues to rise. The current debate in the EU has stressed the need for a cooperative energy security strategy and intensified dialogue with the most important countries in terms of production, transit, and consumption, including China and India. As German Foreign Minister Frank-Walter Steinmeier stated, Europe's goal is "to convince new major consumers of the benefits of functioning energy markets, to avoid problems such as misallocation and reduce risk premiums."[27]

To date, the largest international projects to have been completed are the construction of the Caspian Pipeline Consortium and the Baku-Tbilisi-Ceyhan (BTC) pipelines. The latter project was the most controversial and the most widely discussed. This pipeline was openly supported by the US and equally opposed by Russia. It was presented as a politically driven project rather than an economic one. The project was viewed as commercially non-viable, costly, and further proof of Russia's diminishing influence in the region. Despite this pessimism, the project remains "one of the great engineering endeavours of the new millennium" with the pipeline reaching a length of 1768 km. The pipeline began operating in 2005.[28]

A further ambitious suggestion, backed by the US, is to build an underwater pipeline unlocking Turkmenistan's vast gas resources (most of which are exported exclusively through Russia). This potential project has been constantly discussed without further advancement due to the problem of the legal status of the Caspian. The TransCaspian Pipeline has the potential to be the object of another round of the "Game" of power projection in the region. Russian Industry and Energy Minister Khristenko has said that any decision to build an underwater pipeline will only be possible once the legal status of the Caspian Sea has been determined.[29] The US State Department has already challenged this notion, indicating that it is up to the countries and investors involved to decide whether to proceed.[30] The US policy of decreasing Russian and Iranian influence in the region will continue to further complicate the situation.

No further progress on the issue of the legal status of the Caspian Sea was made at the Special Working Group meeting in Moscow in March. The meeting ended with no conclusive results. This challenge first emerged immediately after the collapse of the Soviet Union and continues to threaten the stability of the region. It also blocks major investments in oil and gas exploration in the Caspian, as the main energy companies are reluctant to take risks in developing disputed areas. Naturally, these companies would prefer to start negotiations on a bilateral basis once ownership rights have been determined.

Another key issue regarding energy security is the protection of pipelines and critical infrastructure. Recent attempted suicide attacks on Saudi oil-processing facilities and attacks on Nigerian oil pipelines by militants show that energy infrastructure is a vulnerable target for terrorist attacks. There is also a threat of sabotage and/or terrorist attacks on the oil and gas infrastructure in the Caspian region. Azerbaijan's Interior Minister has confirmed the existence of such a threat with regard to the BTC pipeline.[31] The situation is even more worrisome when one considers that there are 11 non-state armed groups operating within the Caspian states and further threatening stability in the region.[32]

(c) Environmental Security
All the littoral states are contributing to the repopulation of endangered sturgeon by releasing millions of young fish into the Caspian from sturgeon hatcheries. Despite these measures, the depletion of the population continues to destroy the balance of the ecosystem. The international community has been actively engaged in saving the sturgeon by adopting tough measures, including banning caviar imports and prohibiting export to Western countries. Sadly, violations of the laws and regulations of the littoral states, unprecedented corruption and bureaucracy, and the high levels of poverty and unemployment in the villages on the Caspian's shores make illegal fishing both possible and profitable. In most cases, illegal fishing provides the only source of income for surrounding populations. A number of factors have contributed to the significant depletion of bio-resources in the Caspian region, including the lack of a unified approach to sustainable management of these resources, the lack of effective laws and mechanisms to fight poaching, and the failure of the littoral states to take responsibility for environmental damage.

The main challenge to the environment in the Caspian region is posed by intense oil and gas development and the resulting water pollution through increased oil spills, leaking submerged wells, and waste, which are direct consequences of exploration and drilling operations. The signing of the Tehran Environmental Convention by all the Caspian states was a major step toward protection of the Caspian basin. This agreement recognizes all the acute threats the Caspian ecosystem is currently facing: sea pollution from land-based sources; drilling and seabed mining operations; sea-going vessels; the threat of invasive aquatic species that destroy the ecological balance; and sea-level fluctuations.

3. Dilemmas

The Caspian Sea region faces a number of dilemmas, and regional security will depend on finding solutions to the following problems:

- How to develop mineral resources under the seabed and manage bio-resources in a sustainable manner while at the same time protecting national interests in the absence of an international agreement determining the legal status of the Caspian;

- How to minimize perceived threats among regional and external actors, while at the same time moving toward increasing confidence building and cooperation; and

- How to avoid possible confrontations and conflicts in the Caspian in light of the ongoing militarization of the region.

4. Implications

The Caspian states undoubtedly consider cooperation in dealing with serious regional challenges to be in their strategic interests. Notwithstanding current geopolitical interests, the littoral states and key external powers have pragmatically chosen the path of engagement and cooperation as a means of overcoming problems among them and minimizing real or perceived threats. Still, the absence of a unified Caspian Sea regional organization, with the participation of all littoral states, is a serious impediment to cooperation and regional security.[33] The creation of such a multilateral forum would be a huge step forward in establishing common strategies among the littoral states in responding to new challenges, including fighting terrorism, drug trafficking, WMD proliferation, and avian flu. It would also strengthen trade, economic, and scientific relations.[34] External actors that would benefit from enhanced regional cooperation and integration should encourage the creation of such an organization. Until that happens, bilateral cooperation will continue to be the only effective means of dealing with regional challenges.

As a result of a radical shift in its Caspian policy during Vladimir Putin's presidency, Russia remains a key regional player and has been gradually enhancing its cooperation with all Caspian states. It is currently pursuing a pragmatic approach, making the region a priority in terms of both its domestic and foreign policies. Russia has declared strategic partnerships with all Caspian states on a bilateral basis, which has resulted in an unprecedented increase in bilateral trade, highlighting mutually beneficial economic incentives to enhance further cooperation.[35]

Further developments in the international arena and political changes in key external countries involved will continue to directly affect regional developments. The future direction of intra-state relations will be determined by political and economic developments in the littoral states, China, the European Union, Turkey, and the United States. Despite certain progress, the key risks in the Caspian states continue to be of a political nature. A number of incidents have presented challenges for the political stability that is vital for cooperation and economic prosperity: a series of arrests in Azerbaijan in connection with a planned so-called color revolution by the opposition; the recent strikes of oil workers; the murder of opposition leaders in Kazakhstan and the resulting increased pressure from the international community; Russia's cut-off of exports of natural gas to Ukraine and the resulting supply shortages to Europe; the new law adopted by Turkmenistan granting the president ultimate power in the approval of energy deals and depriving companies of the ability to make independent decisions; and constantly increasing tensions over Iran's nuclear program and referral to the UN Security Council. Unresolved regional conflicts (Nagorno-Karabakh, Abkhazia, South Ossetia, Chechnya) and the undefined status of the Caspian will continue to be factors that hamper and disrupt relations in the region and that prevent the region and neighboring states from enjoying stability and the full benefits of the development of mineral resources.[36]

5. Future Trajectories/Scenarios

The security of the Caspian Sea area as a region of peace, cooperation, and stability remains elusive. It will undoubtedly continue to be one of the world's strategic regions in the immediate future. The existing security architecture could be radically changed by regional conflicts; the continuation of anti-terrorist military operations conducted by the US-led coalition, with the possible deployment of forces in the

Caspian (Azerbaijan); and a probable military strike on Iran's nuclear facilities.[37] In addition, political and governmental changes in the littoral states could bring new approaches to the region that would not necessarily coincide with existing policies.

6. Policy Recommendations

Considering the complexity of Caspian Sea regional security, the following policy recommendations can be applied to ensure stability in the long term:

1. Creation of an organization of the Caspian Sea states that will be based on increased information sharing and that will be a key regional mechanism for dealing with all security challenges;

2. Creation of a common environmental monitoring system, including rapid-reaction units dealing with oil spills (trained personnel and available equipment at ports in the littoral states);

3. Strengthening of multidimensional, regional cooperation (energy, transport infrastructure, trade, security, scientific, and cultural ties), responding to current and futures challenges;

4. Consolidating international efforts in negotiations with Russia, Armenia, Azerbaijan, and Georgia to settle regional conflicts;

5. Prioritizing the resolution of the status of the Caspian Sea on both regional and international levels;

6. Developing regional energy infrastructure to accommodate increased exports of Caspian oil and gas, and diversifying transportation routes offering long-term economic prosperity needed for internal developments in the Caspian states;

7. Prioritizing conservation efforts among the littoral states and adopting unified legal approaches toward fishing regulations;

8. Engaging the littoral states in various internationally funded initiatives to combat drug trafficking, including training programs for law enforcement officials;

9. Building confidence among the regional and extra-regional states toward mutually beneficial cooperation as opposed to a zero-sum approach; and

10. Strengthening regional and international efforts in promoting democracy and good governance in the Caspian, thus investing in long-term internal state stability.

Table 1: Total Catch of Sturgeon in the Caspian Sea (in thousands of tons)[38]

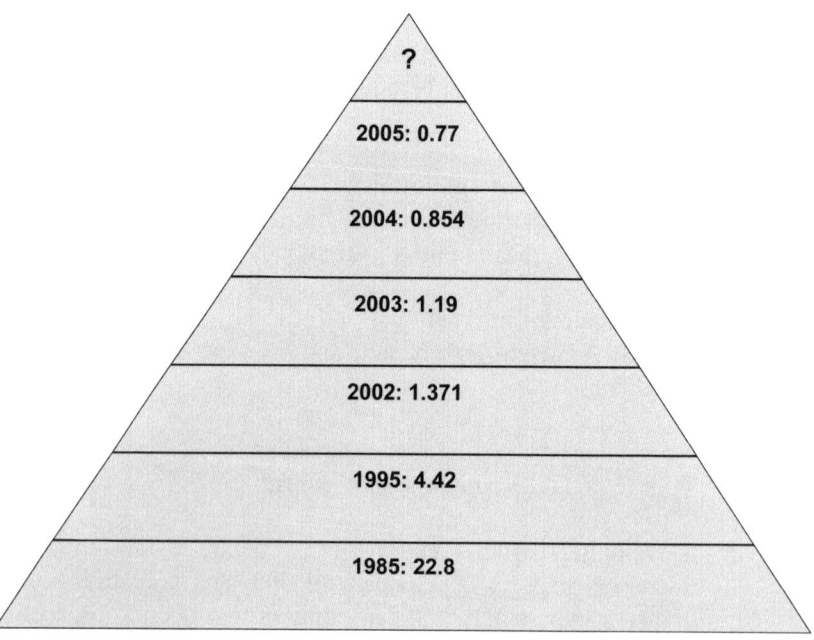

Table 2: Defense Expenditures of the Caspian states (in billions of US dollars)[39]

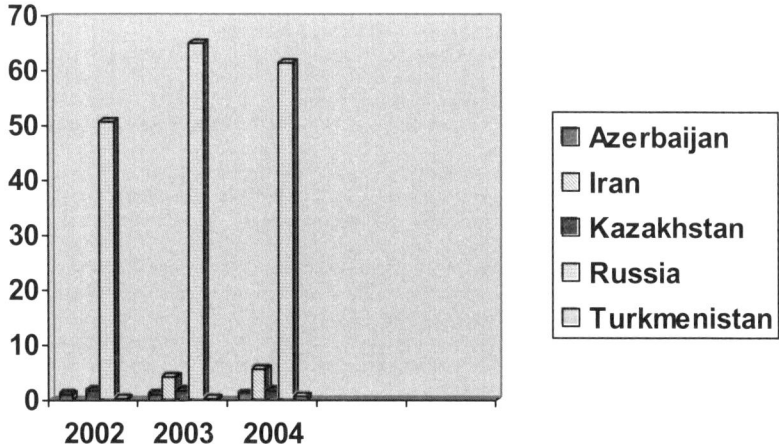

References

[1] The struggle for influence in the region and access to what were at that time the world's first known oil reserves were the ultimate goals of the Great Game between Russia and the British Empire during the 19th century.
[2] In this paper, the terms *Caspian region* or *Caspian* refer to the five independent states bordering the Caspian Sea: Azerbaijan, Iran, Kazakhstan, Russia, and Turkmenistan.
[3] After a series of deadly attacks in 2004, including explosions in the Moscow metro, two simultaneous suicide attacks on commercial airplanes, and a bloody siege of a school in Beslan, Russia managed to prevent a major terrorist attack in 2005. Nevertheless, according to data from the Russian Interior Ministry, 203 terrorism-related incidents were registered in 2005, and 209 attacks were prevented in Chechnya. Statistics can be found on the ministry's website at http://www.mvd.ru/index.php?docid=11.
[4] The full version of the report can be found at http://www.state.gov/p/inl/rls/nrcrpt/2006/vol1/html/62111.htm.
[5] Interview with President George W. Bush by Yaron Deckel, Israeli Television Channel 1, August 11, 2005, http://www.whitehouse.gov/news/releases/2005/08/20050812-2.html.
[6] This applies to a lesser extent to Iran, whose vast oil (third-largest in the world) and gas (second-largest in the world after Russia) reserves are located in the Persian Gulf. Although Iran is planning to expand its oil and gas activities in the Caspian, the region's foremost strategic priority is to help downplay international isolation and counter the US influence.
[7] "Short-term Energy Outlook," Energy Information Administration, March 7, 2006, at http://www.eia.doe.gov/emeu/steo/pub/contents.html.
[8] *Ibid.*
[9] According to Transparency International's Global Corruption Perceptions Index, there has not been much progress in the Caspian states (comparison of figures in the years 2004 and 2005),

placing them in the following order from the least corrupt (according to worldwide ranking): Iran (87/88), Kazakhstan (122/107), Russia (90/126), Azerbaijan (140/137), Turkmenistan (133/155).

[10] President Putin characterized the immense scale of poaching in the Caspian Sea as bio-terrorism during his visit to Astrakhan, in the Caspian region of Russia, in July 2005.

[11] J. Vidal, "Ban on Trade in Wild Caviar as Sturgeon Stocks Plunge," *The Guardian*, January 4, 2006, at http://www.guardian.co.uk/fish/story/01677468,00.html.

[12] The full report can be found at http://www.state.gov/documents/organization/45313.pdf. The US government has been consistent in naming Iran as the most active state sponsor of terrorism, and accusing it of attempting to acquire nuclear weapons.

[13] In 2004, Russia's Caspian Fleet conducted a counterterrorism exercise in Dagestan based on a scenario whereby a terrorist took over a gunship and held hostages (August 25-27, 2004). In 2005, Russia and Kazakhstan conducted a Caspian anti-terrorism exercise (July 28-August 11); Russia and China held a counterterrorism exercise called Peace Mission 2005 (August 18-25, 2005); Russia and India conducted an anti-terrorism exercise called Indra 2005 (October 10-20, 2005) that involved a terrorist attack from the sea and freeing hostages; Turkmenistan conducted its annual anti-terrorism exercise, where, in a simulated scenario, some 3,500 terrorists entered the country (May 2005); Azerbaijan, Georgia, and Turkey conducted a week-long exercise based on a scenario of preventing a terrorist attack against the BTC pipeline (August 2005). In April 2006, Turkmenistan and China signed an agreement on cooperation against extremism, separatism, and terrorism (considering the mutual problem of separatist forces in East Turkestan).

[14] The full version of the *2006 International Narcotics Control Strategy Report* can be found at http://www.state.gov/p/inl/rls/nrcrpt/2006/vol1/html/62111.htm.

[15] An Afghan Opium Survey conducted by the UNODC in 2005 showed that 200 tons of heroin and 1,100 tons of opium were trafficked through Iran. See http://www.unodc.org/pdf/afg/afg_survey_2005_findings.pdf. Iran's security forces have had excellent results in seizing drugs and pursuing an aggressive policy against drug traffickers. It is estimated that more than 3,400 Iranian law enforcement personnel have died in clashes with heavily armed drug traffickers over the last two decades, and Iran reports that another 48 died in 2004. See a US State Department report at http://www.state.gov/p/inl/rls/nrcrpt/2006/vol1/html/62112.htm.

[16] These include the US State Department's Export Control and Border Security program, the Department of Defense's Cooperative Threat Reduction program, the Department of Homeland Security's Container Security Initiative, and the Department of Energy's Second Line of Defense program and its Megaports Initiative, which assist countries in preventing illicit trafficking in nuclear and radiological materials by securing international land borders, seaports, and airports. The Second Line of Defense program and its Megaports Initiative provide special equipment to detect radioactive and nuclear materials at border crossings and seaports and necessary training for law enforcement officials. The Caspian Sea Maritime Interdiction provides equipment for detecting WMD along the maritime borders of Azerbaijan and Kazakhstan and the Caspian Sea. More detailed analysis of the Second Line of Defense program can be found in the author's article "'Vtoraya liniya zashchity': rezul'taty mezhdunarodnogo sotrudnichestva v zone deistviya Astrakhanskoi tamozhni" [Second Line of Defense: Results of International Cooperation in the Zone of Operations of the Astrakhan Customs Service], in '*Yadernyi control*,' No. 3, Fall 2005, pp. 127-144. See http://www.gcsp.ch/E/publications/Issues_Institutions/Russia_CIS/Academic_Papers/Shadrina_PIR_fall05.pdf.

[17] S.L. Quigley, "European Command Transforming to Accommodate New Challenges," American Forces Press Service, March 9, 2006, http://www.defenselink.mil/news/Mar2006/20060309_4440.html.

[18] R. Ismayilov, "Azerbaijan Ponders Russian Caspian Defense Initiative," Eurasia Insight, February 1, 2006, at http://www.eurasianet.org/departments/insight/articles/eav020106.shtml.

[19] Transcript of opening remarks by Russian Foreign Minister Sergey Lavrov at the 20th meeting of the Special Working Group on the Legal Status of the Caspian Sea, Moscow, March 14, 2006, at http://www.mid.ru/brp_4.nsf/e78a48070f128a7b43256999005bcbb3/d02103c9696b6deac325

7132002504f7?OpenDocument.
[20] "Stability in Central Asia serves Iran national security," IRNA, November 8, 2005, at http://www.iranmania.com/News/ArticleView/Default.asp?NewsCode=37535&NewsKind=Current%20Affairs.
[21] Lavrov, *op. cit.*, note 19.
[22] *Ibid.*
[23] In 2001, an Iranian patrol boat threatened to use force and ordered an Azerbaijani ship with experts from British Petroleum to leave the area of the disputed oil fields (both Azerbaijan and Iran claim ownership).
[24] J.T. Correll, "European Command Looks South and East," Air Force Magazine Online, December 2003, at http://www.afa.org/magazine/dec2003/1203eucom.asp.
[25] "India, China Plans for Oil Cooperation at Early Stage," AFX News Limited, August 26, 2005.
[26] "Russia to Sharply Increase Oil and Gas Exports to Asia-Pacific – Minister," *Moscow News*, February 22, 2006, at http://www.mosnews.com/money/2006/02/22/asiafuelexports.shtml.
[27] F. Steinmeier, "Avoiding Conflict Over Fuel," *International Herald Tribune*, March 22, 2006, at http://www.iht.com/articles/2006/03/22/opinion/edstein.php.
[28] "Baku-Tbilisi-Ceyhan Pipeline Overview," BP Caspian, at http://www.bp.com/genericarticle.do?categoryId=9006669&contentId=7014358.
[29] Viktor Khristenko: "Submerged pipelines' construction is possible only after determination of the legal status of the Caspian Sea," Azerbaijan Today, February 23, 2006, at http://www.today.az/news/business/23580.html.
[30] Matt Bryza, Deputy Assistant Secretary of State for European and Eurasian Affairs, February 22, 2006.
[31] "We Are Determined to Provide Security for Our Country and Its Strategic Infrastructure," Interview with Lt. Gen. Eldar Mahmudov, National Security Minister of Azerbaijan, *Caspian Energy (Russia)*, Vol. 34, No. 6, 2005, at http://www.mns.gov.az/musahibe_8_en.html.
[32] The data is based on Table 57, "Selected Non-State Armed Groups," *The Military Balance* (London: Routledge, 2006), pp. 418-434
[33] In 1992, Iran proposed the creation of the Caspian Sea Cooperation Organisation, which was to be supported by all the littoral states. Up until now, however, the initiative exists on paper only.
[34] Avian flu, which is now spreading widely in the region, has emerged as a new threat and has revealed a new aspect of cooperation among the littoral states: fighting infectious diseases. All Caspian countries have confirmed cases of avian flu, while Azerbaijan has even had human casualties.
[35] In 2005, bilateral trade turnover between Russia and Kazakhstan reached nearly $10 billion (35 percent more than in 2004); trade between Russia and Azerbaijan increased by 40 percent to $1.06 billion; trade between Russia and Iran was $2.05 billion; and trade with Turkmenistan was $300.6 million. Official data on Russia's trade turnover with foreign countries can be found on the website of the Russian Federal Customs Service, at http://www.customs.ru/ru/stats/arhiv-stats-new/popup.php?id286=125.
[36] The negotiations were sparked by a statement on the Nagorno-Karabakh conflict by Azerbaijani President Ilham Aliyev to the effect that peace talks cannot last forever and that the patience of the Azerbaijani people and government was running out. See A. Babayan and J. Peuch, "Nagorno-Karabakh: Russia Calls for 'Mutually-Acceptable Solution'," Radio Free Europe/Radio Liberty, April 6, 2006, at http://www.rferl.org/featuresarticle/2006/04/6825b16b-8fc1-41f6-88ce-89484c98818f.html.
[37] For more information on possible US deployment in the Caspian, see "Options for Changing the Army's Overseas Basing," report by the US Congressional Budget Office, May 2004, http://www.cbo.gov/ftpdocs/54xx/doc5415/05-03-ArmyOBasing.pdf.
[38] V.P. Ivanov, "Biologicheskie resursy Kaspiiskogo Morya" [Biological Resources of the Caspian Sea] (Astrakhan: KaspNIRKH, 2000); reports and press releases of the Caspian Fisheries Research Institute, at http://www.caspnirh.astranet.ru.

[39] Data was taken from Table 44, "Comparative Defence Expenditures and Military Manpower, 2002-2004," *The Military Balance* (London: Routledge, 2006), pp.398-400.

CHAPTER 5

EDITORIAL OF POLICY BRIEF ON SECURITY IN THE
CASPIAN SEA REGION: CHALLENGES AND
OPPORTUNITIES IN A GLOBALIZED WORLD

NAYEF R.F. AL-RODHAN

Dr. Nayef R.F. Al-Rodhan is Senior Scholar in Geostrategy and Director of the Program on the Geopolitical Implications of Globalization and Transnational Security at the Geneva Centre for Security Policy, Geneva, Switzerland

1. Review and Critique

The Caspian Sea region broadly includes the five states of Central Asia and the three states of the South Caucasus and Russia. After the collapse of the Soviet Union, the Caspian Sea region attracted a considerable amount of international attention, due to its sizable energy reserves as well as its geostrategic position between Europe and Asia, with neighbors that include Iran and Turkey. It has since become an arena of regional, as well as global, competition over the development and transportation of mineral resources, as well as influence in the Caucasus and Central Asia. As Ekaterina Shadrina notes in her brief, the region's large hydrocarbon resources make it one of the most promising energy sources of the United States (US), the European Union (EU), China, Turkey, and India.[1]

The region's largely untapped energy reserves would appear to augur well for its future. Yet, the geopolitical weight of the Caspian Sea region is also accompanied by a number of threats to stability. The Caspian states are fragile ones that are currently struggling with difficult economic and political transitions. They continue to suffer from weak institutions that lack the capacity to fulfill basic political, economic, and social functions. There is also a perceptible criminalization of the structures of authority, as well as widespread corruption.[2] These factors add up to an extremely fragile security situation, since destabilizing domestic and regional ethnic tensions so often lie just below the surface.

Shadrina observes that the region's stability is tenuous for a number of reasons. Unresolved regional conflicts, including the Nagorno-Karabakh enclave in Azerbaijan, secessionist movements in Georgia, the extremely unstable situation in Afghanistan, and Russia's on-going conflict in Chechnya continue to cast a shadow over the region. Moreover, the Caspian Sea region's location – at the crossroads between Western Europe, East Asia, and the Middle East – serves as a transit route for trafficking of weapons of mass destruction and drugs, as well as terrorists.[3] Weak state institutions complicate the challenge of effectively addressing these transnational security issues.

The Caspian Sea's ecosystem is also in danger of being sacrificed at the expense of energy wealth. Offshore drilling is believed to have a negative effect on the environment at every stage of production. Seismic-testing, entailing underwater explosions, can injure and kill marine life. The by-products of drilling, as well as accidental oil spills, cause further damage to marine animals and plants, while introducing toxins into the food supply of both animals and humans.[4] In addition, the "other black gold" – black caviar-bearing sturgeon – are also under threat, another point raised by Shadrina. The Caspian's sturgeon population is in decline, due to poaching and catastrophic levels of over-fishing. Moreover, the expansion of drilling for petroleum is also likely to place these endangered sturgeon under increased threat.

2. Dilemmas and Our Recommendations

Thus, while the Caspian Sea region is rich in oil and natural gas reserves, the region's future is held hostage to a number of unresolved conflicts, ethnic tensions, religious extremism, and environmental damage and degradation. Weak state institutions also make the task of managing such issues even more challenging. Below, we suggest eight dilemmas or challenges facing policy makers, as well as eight corresponding recommendations.

A major challenge facing policy makers in the region is how to balance the economic gains from energy resources against the risk of over-exploitation and environmental degradation. In order to safeguard the long-term economic security of the region, as well to ensure greater environmental security, regulations should be put in place to protect natural resources. Preventing over-fishing of sturgeon is also in the long-term interests of the region. Fish quotas should be strictly enforced, and yearly assessments of fish stocks should take place.

The extraction and transportation of energy reserves from the Caspian Sea region is a major source of geopolitical rivalry. Pipeline routes proposed by companies linked to non-regional powers are controversial because they are aimed at limiting the influence of Russia and neighboring Iran in the region. Russia and Iran, however, are also eager to have oil and gas from the region pass through their territories.[5] Policy makers in the region are, therefore, confronted with the dilemma of advantages of transnational pipelines and the geopolitics of their installation. Agreements between states in the region must outline economic and political details to ensure equality of costs and benefits.

Another challenge is linked to the intervention of non-regional actors in regional conflicts. Outside concerns about regional conflicts may be driven by commercial or strategic motivations. This being the case, external involvement may even serve to exacerbate rather than ameliorate political, ethnic, and religious tensions in the region.[6]

In order to be effective in addressing crime, terrorism, and non-state actors, the Caspian states will need to collaborate in the security domain. Regional cooperation is, therefore, needed to help cope with a whole host of security challenges, including those linked to the environment, regional conflicts, as well as terrorism, drug trafficking and the proliferation of weapons of mass destruction. The success of regional security arrangements will depend on the role of Russia.

3. Conclusion

Thus, while the Caspian Sea region is rich in oil and gas reserves, a number of factors make it unstable, including ongoing regional conflicts and the geopolitical interests of outside powers. The region's position between Western Europe, East Asia, and the Middle East also make it a prime transit area for non-state actors engaged in illicit activities. Unfortunately, the Caspian states weak institutional capacities make the task of dealing with an array of transnational security challenges extremely complex.

References

[1] For the brief in its entirety, please see Chapter 4.
[2] V. (Ze'ev) Khanin, "Clientelism, Corruption and the Struggle for Power in Central Asia: The Case of Kyrgystan," in M. Gammer, *The Caspian Region*, Vol. 1 (London and New York: Routledge, 2004).
[3] See J.H. Kalicki, "Caspian Energy at the Crossroads," *Foreign Affairs*, Vol. 80, No. 5, September/October 2001.
[4] R.E. Neville, "Two Black Golds: Petroleum Extraction and Environmental Protection in the Caspian Sea," *Journal of Public and International Affairs*, Vol. 12, Spring 2001, pp. 110-111.
[5] See S. Alam, "Pipeline Politics in the Caspian Sea Basin," *Strategic Analysis: A Monthly Journal of IDSA*, January-March 2002.
[6] V. Rubin, "The Geopolitics of Energy Development in the Caspian Region: Regional Cooperation or Conflict?,"*Conference Report*, Center for International Security and Cooperation, Stanford University, December 1999, p. 17.

CHAPTER 6

PREVENTION OF WMD PROLIFERATION,
GLOBALIZATION, AND INTERNATIONAL SECURITY

VLADIMIR ORLOV

Dr. Vladimir Orlov is Course Co-Director of the European Training Course in Security Policy at the Geneva Centre for Security Policy, Geneva, Switzerland

Abstract
The proliferation of weapons of mass destruction is probably the most urgent threat to international security in the 21st century. The author analyzes the current status of the international non-proliferation regime in a new, globalized system of international relations; looks at case studies (Iran, North Korea, Pakistan, India, and non-state actors); and, based on his more than 15 years of experience in the field, provides policy recommendations on how to reduce the risk of proliferation in the near- and mid-term future.

1. Policy Challenges

Iran's nuclear ambitions, six-party talks on North Korea's nuclear-weapons program, the controversial nuclear deal between the United States (US) and India, modernization of China's strategic nuclear forces, attempts by major international terrorist networks to get access to weapons of mass destruction (WMD) or their most sensitive components: these are all realities of today's political scene. And these realities are attracting increased attention by the world media. The word *nuclear*, by default, adds flavor to news columns or to op-eds. And the abbreviation "WMD," which until recently had been exclusively a part of the vocabulary of experts, is today used by anyone who has access to a television or reads newspapers. WMD was one of the key terms used on the eve of the US-led war against Iraq in 2003, when the general public was invited, trough the media, to follow the hunt for Saddam's *hidden WMDs*, a hunt that never achieved its declared goal, that could not, as Saddam had no WMDs to hunt for.

The above example shows one of the major risks of the globalized world and of the worldwide impact of the international media: stories about WMD proliferation make front-page news, which increases the sale of newspapers, and they also lead to political declarations, which can help sell wars to the general public.

***

WMD proliferation should be, with little doubt, included in any list of the most urgent global threats to international security in the 21st century. As Russian President Vladimir Putin once said, "proliferation is probably *the* most urgent threat [of all]."[1]

The Nuclear Non-Proliferation Treaty (NPT), which came into force in 1970, is intended to act as the main barrier against the threat of proliferation. This treaty is unique, considering the number of parties that belong to it.[2] Other treaties dealing with the threat of proliferation include the Convention on the Prohibition of Chemical Weapons (CWC) (1993), the Biological Weapons Convention (BWC) (1974), and the Comprehensive Nuclear Test Ban Treaty (concluded in 1996 but not yet in force). Antarctica, the South Pacific, Latin America, the Caribbean, Africa, and Southeast Asia have been declared nuclear-weapons-free zones. The International Atomic Energy Agency (IAEA), established almost 50 years ago, plays a leading role among the international organizations that are now combating nuclear proliferation. The United Nations (UN) Security Council has the power to impose sanctions against countries that violate the non-proliferation regime. This is what the international non-proliferation architecture looks like, at least on paper. But how do things actually stand?

The term "international treaty" is no longer very popular in some capitals. Instead, they propose using alternative methods, such as an *ozirak* policy. This refers to preventive attacks against countries suspected of proliferating WMD, and it takes its name from an attack by Israel in 1981, when it bombed Iraq's Tammuz I nuclear reactor near the town of Ozirak. This is the type of action taken by the US in 1998, when it launched a missile attack against a facility in Sudan that was suspected of being related to Osama Bin Laden's biological-weapons program. The reality, however, has been disappointing for those claiming to "expose regimes," and it contradicts their statements that agreements no longer work.

Today, there are 8 ½ countries that possess nuclear weapons: the five nuclear states as recognized by the NPT (China, France, the United Kingdom, Russia, and the United States); three states that have nuclear weapons but that have refrained from joining the NPT (India and Pakistan, which have carried out successful nuclear tests, and Israel, whose nuclear arsenal is comparable, according to some estimates, to that of the United Kingdom or France[3]); and the remaining "half" is North Korea. This country has come so close to developing nuclear weapons that, before the ink has dried on this policy memo, it may be necessary to change 8 ½ to 9. Moreover, North Korea's leadership declared a year ago already that it is in fact a new nuclear-weapon state. The information presently available suggests, however, that it is still too early to classify North Korea as a de facto nuclear-weapon state.

(a) Are 8½ too few or too many?
From the point of view of general and complete nuclear disarmament (the goal established in Article VI of the NPT), this number is too high. The NPT aims to gradually reduce the number of countries that possess nuclear weapons, not to mention reducing and ultimately eliminating nuclear weapons altogether. But if we take a realistic view of how things stand, we would have to admit that the number of nuclear-weapon states might actually be as high as several dozen.

According to the Pentagon's 1963 estimates, which were recently declassified, at least 10 countries could have developed nuclear weapons – together with the means for delivering them – in under 10 years. But, "for some reason," Australia, Argentina, Brazil, Romania, Sweden, and Switzerland terminated their nuclear-weapons programs.[4] South Africa voluntarily gave up the nuclear weapons it had developed. Belarus, Kazakhstan, and Ukraine agreed to return all nuclear weapons from their territories to Russia following the collapse of the Soviet Union. Over the last decade, more countries have joined the NPT, among them Argentina, Brazil, China, Cuba, France, and Ukraine.

The NPT has not always been the reason why countries have given up their nuclear ambitions. Yet the NPT has kept states from making political decisions on the development of nuclear weapons of their own; such decisions would have undermined the existing non-proliferation regime, thus provoking a dangerous chain reaction in various regions of the world. The NPT has established the rules of the game and made clear the advantages of maintaining a non-nuclear status, while ensuring the strict interdependence of the participating states.

In another area of concern, you could not count on one hand the number of states that now possess other types of WMD, most notably, chemical and biological weapons. These weapons, especially chemical ones, are easier and cheaper to make; they can be reasonably described as the A-bomb for the poor. Whereas the CWC provides for verification mechanisms for the participating states, the BWC lacks such a mechanism, and the work on a protocol for this mechanism has stalled.

The number of countries that possess missile weapons has been growing at the fastest rate in comparison with those that possess nuclear, biological, and chemical weapons. This is because of so-called secondary proliferation when, for example, North Korea, Pakistan, and Iran established mutual ties. International agreements do not prohibit the development of delivery vehicles. Furthermore, the "gentleman's agreements" between major producers of missile equipment and technologies, known as the Missile Technology Control Regime, can slow down, but not prevent, the development of missile programs in countries with such ambitions. Yet the most important goal of checking the proliferation of nuclear weapons has been successful to date.

(b) North Korea
North Korea provides a classic example of non-compliance with NPT obligations.

Considering North Korea's nuclear and missile capabilities, together with the veil of secrecy surrounding its regime and its unpredictability, one should admit that this country is a serious instability factor both for Northeast Asia and the world. However, a diplomatic solution to the North Korean problem seems quite possible. It could be found on a multilateral basis, perhaps on two levels at once.

The first level is the six-party mechanism (including both Koreas, China, Japan, Russia, and the US), which could help draft a document, even a non-binding one, that would include North Korea's pledge to return to the NPT and to open up all of its territory for unconditional IAEA inspections.

Other issues that could be discussed include economic, energy, and other aid packages to Pyongyang from the above-mentioned countries and the European Union (EU), as well as the issue of missile non-proliferation. Simultaneously, or perhaps later, both Koreas must confirm the Korean Peninsula's nuclear-free status and receive guarantees from the nuclear powers.

The second level should be bilateral North Korea-US dialogue and should lead toward security assurances for North Korea from the US. It is clear, however, that, at least for now, the US administration is not ready for this.

(c) Iran
Unlike North Korea, Iran is a party to the NPT and is an active member of the IAEA. So far, there is no definite proof that Iran has developed or is developing nuclear weapons.

The situation concerning Iran and the question of non-proliferation boils down to the ability to make an accurate forecast for the next three to five years. During this period, Iran will probably be able to transfer its ambitious civilian nuclear power program to military purposes, if its leadership decides to make such a political decision. This probability must not be allowed: if Iran possesses nuclear weapons, together with modern delivery vehicles, it would constitute a threat to global and regional security and international stability.

Few question the idea that Iran has a military nuclear program. In 1993, Russia's foreign intelligence reported that Iran "ha[d] a program for military applied research in the nuclear field." The report went on and stated that, without outside technological and research assistance, the appearance of nuclear weapons in Iran before 2001 was unlikely; and even if Iran invested some $1.5 billion in its nuclear program every year, it would not be able to develop nuclear weapons earlier than 2003.[5]

Three years ago, my colleagues at the Moscow-based PIR Center, having assessed all of the information concerning Iran's advanced nuclear program, arrived at the following conclusion: factors that may have caused Iran to accelerate its nuclear program include its wish to: "obtain technical capabilities for developing nuclear weapons. In this case, Iran could go very far, while remaining within the framework of its international commitments... According to such a scenario, Tehran could receive technical and material capabilities for developing nuclear weapons within months, as soon as it accumulates the required amount of weapons-grade nuclear materials. A political decision to use resources of nuclear materials for developing nuclear weapons can be made if Iranian-US relations become aggravated and the US starts preparing an operation to overthrow the incumbent regime in Iran, or if the US or Israel bombs Iranian nuclear facilities..."[6]

When assessing the current situation in Iran, many experts believe that the world must recognize the existence of a dichotomy.

On the one hand, because Iran is a proud nation that wants to stand on equal footing with the most technologically advanced states, it will develop its nuclear energy, space exploration, and biotechnology programs at almost any cost. On the other hand, Iran's leadership has repeatedly proven itself to be untrustworthy. In recent years, the international community has witnessed a variety of falsehoods from Iran about its nuclear program. Yet this history of deception does not necessarily mean that Iran has decided to produce nuclear weapons.

Now the question arises: is Tehran deliberately maintaining uncertainty about its plans (the way its sworn enemy Israel has done, thus keeping its nuclear policy under a shroud of complete secrecy) in order to broaden its room for further bargaining? Or do the Iranians themselves not know what they should do next? The latter thesis seems more probable. Iran's elites seem to be divided over the question of the direction of their civilian nuclear program, and how it should be developed, with whom and how they should bargain (and whether they should bargain at all) over a possibility of Iran's giving up its nuclear-weapons ambitions? And most important, what should they demand in return for their cooperation?

The Iranian leadership obviously includes groups that hope for a strategic rapprochement with the US. Washington displays less interest in such a scenario, yet some policy makers there seem interested. Both countries are now maintaining rigid positions, so that they can later reduce the stakes, while leaving a lot of room for bargaining and, ultimately, for a compromise. Tehran does not have a unified US policy, nor does Washington have a unified Iran policy. This factor reduces the possibility for bargaining but does not rule it out.

(d) Pakistan
For me, Pakistan presents the greatest international proliferation-related concern today.

First, Pakistan has already demonstrated that it is a real, not virtual, proliferator. Through Dr. A.Q. Khan's led international network, Pakistan provided nuclear-weapons-related materials and knowledge (including even the design of nuclear weapons) to such states as North Korea, Iran, and Libya. It is known that, in 1990, assistance in building nuclear-weapons capabilities was offered by the Khan network to Saddam Hussein (who refused to accept it thinking, wrongly so, that it was an American provocation). It is not publicly known yet what other states might have received Khan's nuclear "services" or had other kinds of similar arrangements with Pakistan's government. (Pakistan's government has never officially recognized that it had been informed about Khan's illegal activities, and it has never allowed the IAEA or other internationally recognized groups of inspectors or investigators to independently interrogate Dr. Khan).

Second, the level of security of Pakistan's nuclear arsenal provides room for a number of questions. Pakistan's warheads are widely believed to be demated, that is, the highly enriched uranium (HEU) has been removed from the rest of the weapon. Security analysts generally believe that this is a safer means of storing warheads, particularly in such an unstable and terrorist- or extremist-filled region. The most recent analyses prove, however, that demated weapons may pose a greater threat than mated warheads. According to these analyses, short of terrorists enlisting insider assistance to teach them how to detonate a fully assembled nuclear weapon, they would have more confidence in exploding bombs they build themselves. Another advantage for terrorists is that presently almost all of Pakistan's nuclear weapons are powered with HEU. By stealing the HEU, which is being stored separately from demated warheads, terrorists would have the material they would need to build the simplest, improvised nuclear device.[7]

(e) India
The current international debate on India's nuclear program brings qualitatively new elements to international non-proliferation-related debates on the whole.

Being, legally, in the same position as Pakistan or Israel as a non-member of the NPT and, consequently, with its nuclear-weapons status not recognized by the international community, India, unlike the two other states, recently managed in three or four years to achieve what could be viewed by the non-proliferation purists as *impossible*: de facto recognition as the sixth full member of the nuclear club.

To be precise, the recognition process has just started, and it will take a considerable amount of time to make it a part of international norms. But with three of the permanent five members of the UN Security Council – France, Russia, and the United States – in favor, though to different degrees, of accepting India's nuclear status, the situation will now change rapidly. The US-India nuclear agreement of July 2005 was only a modest preface in advance of a full revision of India's role in the nuclear world. But it definitely boosted the whole process of bringing India into the club, and now it is more a question of time rather than of general direction.[8]

With its maturing nuclear arsenal and dramatically increasing missile capabilities, India, which is not an NPT member state, is joining the nuclear club and enjoying its privileges free from significant limiting commitments or pressures.

(f) Non-state actors

I have been studying the phenomenon of the interest of violent non-state actors in WMD and their components for more than a decade. During this time, it has become clear that the key question has shifted from *whether* terrorists are willing to use weapons of mass destruction to *when* and *how* this will happen.

Technological development has made it possible for major international terrorist networks – those with extensive financial and intellectual resources – to eventually succeed in acquiring or producing WMD components and, as a result, to commit a spectacular terrorist attack with resulting mass destruction.

While access to, and detonation of, a nuclear warhead still seems to be a highly unlikely scenario (perhaps only Pakistan could be the source for such an operation, as already discussed above) even for the most advanced terrorist organizations, sabotage of highly sensitive nuclear facilities (including, but not limited to, nuclear power plants), access to considerable amounts of HEU, or production of an improvised nuclear device are all *real and present dangers*. For less advanced terrorist networks, an attack on a major metropolitan area using biological weapons could be the most attractive scenario, and preparations for such attacks have been detected in places like Waziristan (Pakistan/Afghanistan) and the Pankisi Gorge (Georgia).

2. Responses

The good news is that there is still a wide variety of options for the international community to respond both to traditional proliferation threats (involving state actors) and to non-traditional ones (involving non-state actors).

Among such responses, the following are the ones cited most often:

A. A combination of legal and practical steps aimed at strengthening the nuclear non-proliferation regime:

- Put a five-year hold on the construction of additional facilities for uranium enrichment and plutonium separation. There is no compelling reason to build more of these facilities, as the nuclear industry has more than enough capacity to fuel its power plants and research centers. To make this holding period acceptable to everyone, get the countries that already have the facilities to commit to guaranteeing a supply of nuclear fuel for bona fide uses. Then use the hiatus to develop better long-term options for managing the technologies (for example, in regional centers under multinational control).

- Speed up existing efforts to modify research reactors worldwide that are operating with HEU, particularly those with metal fuel that could be readily employed as bomb material. Convert these reactors to use low-enriched uranium, and accelerate research on how to make HEU unnecessary for all peaceful nuclear applications.

- Raise the bar for inspection standards by establishing the "Additional Protocol" to safeguard agreements with the IAEA as the norm for verifying compliance with the NPT. Without the expanded authority of this protocol, the IAEA's inspection rights are limited. It has proven its value recently in Iran and Libya and should be brought into force for all countries.

- Call on the United Nations Security Council to act swiftly and decisively in the case of any country that withdraws from the NPT, in terms of the threat the withdrawal poses to international peace and security.

- Urge states to act on UN Security Council Resolution 1540 (April 2004) to pursue and prosecute any illicit trading in nuclear material and technology.[9]

B. Counterproliferation measures:

- Strengthening of national and international systems of export controls in relation to sensitive materials and technologies (including intangible technology transfers), stopping any suspicious transfers in accordance with the "catch-all" principle;

- Preventing states of concern and particularly violent non-state actors from gaining access to weapons-grade materials, as well as to teams of skilled nuclear scientists and engineers. The Proliferation Security Initiative can play a significant role, particularly when detentions of ships at sea are concerned; and

- Destroying facilities for WMD production.

I argue that: (a) only a combination of measures can bring fruitful results in combating proliferation; and (b) each case of proliferation concern is unique, i.e. no *general rules* exist that are applicable to situations as different as Iran, North Korea, and Pakistan, or non-state actors.

3. Dilemmas

There are at least four major dilemmas the international community currently faces in regard to WMD proliferation:

- First (relating particularly to India), whether the NPT should be treated as a foundation of international security that cannot be altered, even if needed; or whether a set of practical measures can be undertaken to complement the NPT and, to a certain extent, to start building a new regime that meets the challenges of a new century;

- Second (relating particularly to Iran), whether any state participating in the nuclear non-proliferation regime can be deprived of its right to develop peaceful nuclear technologies simply as a result of others' suspicions of its intentions, whether the right to benefit from new technologies and technological development can be monopolized by a few traditional players in the international arena;

- Third (relating particularly to Iran, as well as North Korea to a certain extent), whether sanctions, even if legally approved by the UN Security Council, can be a useful tool for the containment of nuclear military programs and/or intentions, or whether they will only irritate countries subject to sanctions, causing them to move toward complete isolation and non-transparency and, at the same time, helping to consolidate public opinion within that nation in support of its regime;

- Fourth (relating particularly to non-state actors, as well as to certain state actors, like Pakistan), whether preventive military operations that destroy WMD-related sites, stop suspicious activities, or allow dangerous weapons to be seized and removed from this or that country can help reduce global proliferation risks, or whether they will be unable to eliminate sources of proliferation.

4. Future Scenarios

This section includes descriptions of possible scenarios of proliferation-driven developments in the world in the next five to ten years:

(a) Scenario A: Nothing will change
As a result of the efforts of the international community (mostly multilateral, but combined with certain unilateral initiatives by the permanent five members of the UN Security Council), the number of

states with nuclear weapons stabilizes. The list of states of concern will be similar or even the same as it is now. Iran will temporarily freeze its full-scale nuclear enrichment in exchange for European "carrots" and US security assurances. North Korea will continue bargaining but will never test its nuclear weapons, which will raise questions about whether it really has them or is only blackmailing the international community. Thanks to the strengthening of export controls, internationally and nationally, along with strong efforts to improve the physical protection of fissile materials, terrorists will fail to successfully commit a major WMD terrorist act, though a terrorist act involving chemical or radiological weapons may take place, in Europe or in East Asia.

(b) Scenario B: Success story
The international community, under pressure from deteriorating proliferation-related developments, agrees on a set of measures to strengthen the NPT and the whole non-proliferation regime. Iran, under international pressure and as a result of domestic calculations, renounces its advanced nuclear program in exchange for full-scale cooperation with Europe and the United States. North Korea returns to the NPT as a non-nuclear-weapon state, destroys its weapons-grade stocks under IAEA supervision, opens up its economy, and works with South Korea on a reunification plan. Russia and the US sign the Moscow-2 Treaty on significant reductions in their arsenals of strategic nuclear weapons, as well as in their arsenals of non-strategic weapons. As a result of intelligence sharing, the labs of terrorists working on the preparation of a biological or radiological attack are destroyed by preventive missile strikes. The new government in Israel agrees to start talks, with no preconditions, on establishing a zone free of WMD in the Middle East.

(c) Scenario C: Collapse
Thanks to international sanctions, Iran's leadership consolidates its power domestically and advances toward building nuclear weapons. US strikes on Iran's nuclear facilities fail to destroy most of them and leads to an impeachment in the White House. But Iran does not want to maintain dialogue with other forces in the US or in Europe and tests its nuclear weapons, declaring itself a new nuclear-weapon state. In regional response, Egypt declares that it is developing nuclear weapons. Pakistan provides Saudi Arabia with a dozen ready-to-

detonate nuclear devices and with teams of engineers for technical support. Turkey, frustrated both by the regional developments and by its non-acceptance in the EU, withdraws from a declining NATO and rapidly develops its own nuclear-weapons capabilities, supported by scientists and engineers from Russia, its new closest ally. In East Asia, North and South Korea merge, with the North's nuclear weapons and missiles and with the South's technological and financial capabilities. In response, Japan renounces its nuclear-weapons-free status and produces plutonium-based nuclear weapons within five weeks of its declaration. Nobody remembers what NPT stands for.

(d) Scenario D: Something will change, but not much
This is the same as scenario A, but with three major developments. First, India is officially invited by the Security Council's permanent five to have observer status in relation to the NPT, de facto recognizing its nuclear-weapons status. The "Nuclear Five" becomes "5+1" and later the "Nuclear Six." Second, with domestic instability in Pakistan increasing, the US, Russia, and China implement a joint operation: US Special Forces seize and remove Pakistan's nuclear devices, which had been previously decoded; China provides its territory for "temporary storage;" and, finally, the weapons are dismantled in Russia, where the fissile materials are stored. Third, six-party talks result in the denuclearization of North Korea, mostly thanks to China's efforts, and in extensive international assistance programs to Pyongyang.

How realistic are these scenarios? In terms of probability I would rank them D – A – C – B, in which D is the mostly likely scenario and B is the least likely The situation is, however, very fragile, and any significant proliferation-related crisis could change the ranking toward C – D – A – B.

5. Policy Recommendations

1. On the global level, the international community (through NPT review conferences and through the IAEA) should adopt a set of measures to strengthen the nuclear non-proliferation regime as proposed in the section "Responses."

2. On Iran and North Korea, the security concerns of these nations should be taken into consideration. Security assur-

ances should be provided to them, under international patronage, as well as international technical assistance, including in nuclear energy projects, but under strict international (special no-limit IAEA inspections) control.

3. On Pakistan, the situation should be monitored with increased attention with regard to the capability of the government to provide adequate security for its nuclear arsenal.

4. On Israel and the Middle East, the US, France, and Russia should strongly encourage Israel to agree, with no preconditions, to start negotiations with its neighbors on establishing of a zone free of WMD in the Middle East.

5. On attempts by terrorists to get access to WMD and use them, there is little that can be done on the international or national levels. However, the most urgent steps should include: further increasing the physical protection of critical infrastructure, including nuclear facilities; improving export controls internationally and nationally; improving customs and border controls; exchanging information on terrorists' activities and intentions; making preventive strikes on terrorists' WMD labs, when there is reliable information about them; and carrying out regular international simulations and exercises on reducing the consequences of WMD terrorist attacks.

6. On India: it is already de facto a member of the nuclear club. And it is a reliable player. It should be formally brought into the club and should agree on acceptance of the NPT norms.

7. On nuclear weapons: Russia and the US should agree, in the near future, to reduce the levels of their strategic nuclear arsenals to around 1,000 warheads each. Further on, the Security Council permanent five should hold talks on further reductions, with obligations by all nuclear-weapons states (including India) not to increase the numbers of their nuclear arsenals and to negotiate gradual reductions.

References

[1] Breakfast with Frost TV Interview with President Putin, broadcast on June 22, 2003.
[2] India, Israel, and Pakistan are not parties to the NPT. North Korea has withdrawn from the NPT.
[3] See, V. Malevannyi, "Israel's Intelligence Community" (original title appeared in Russian) *Nezavisimoe voennoe obozrenie*, May 15-22, 1998, p. 7. In contrast to Malevannyi, I hold that Israel tends to exaggerate rather than understate the size of its military nuclear program.
[4] R.M. Timerbaev, *Russia and Nuclear Non-Proliferation* (original title appeared in Russian) (Moscow: Nauka, 1999), pp. 137-161, p. 172.
[5] "New Post-Cold War Challenge: Proliferation of Weapons of Mass Destruction" (original title appeared in Russian) (Moscow: Foreign Intelligence Service of the Russian Federation, 1993).
[6] V.F. Lata, A.V. Khlopkov, "Iran: Nuclear and Missile Puzzle for Russia," 'Yaderny Kontrol,' No. 2, Issue 68, 2003, p. 45.
[7] C.D. Ferguson, "Preventing Catastrophic Nuclear Terrorism," Special Report by the Council on Foreign Relations, No.11, March 2006, pp. 12-13.
[8] See R. Einhorn, "Nuclear Rapprochement between India and the U.S.: Pros and Cons" (original title appeared in Russian), '*Yaderny Kontrol*,' No. 4, 2005, pp.75-82.
[9] M. ElBaradei, "Seven Steps to Raise World Security," *Financial Times*, February 2, 2005.

CHAPTER 7

EDITORIAL OF POLICY BRIEF ON PREVENTION OF
WMD PROLIFERATION, GLOBALIZATION, AND
INTERNATIONAL SECURITY

NAYEF R.F. AL-RODHAN

Dr. Nayef R.F. Al-Rodhan is Senior Scholar in Geostrategy and Director of the Program on the Geopolitical Implications of Globalization and Transnational Security at the Geneva Centre for Security Policy, Geneva, Switzerland

1. Review and Critique

Many academics and analysts argue that one of the most pressing issues facing global security today is the prevention of the proliferation of weapons of mass destruction (WMD), including limiting the proliferation of their components and delivery systems. This has certainly become an issue for the larger globalization debate and represents an area where there is a pressing need for the international community to engage, especially given recent key developments by potential nuclear states to arm themselves militarily with WMD and ongoing negotiations with other states regarding nuclear programs.

Since the Nuclear Non-Proliferation Treaty (NPT) came into force in 1970, the world has advanced further toward a nuclear-free status. However, in the past couple of decades, with the fall of the Soviet Union, the rising military force of China, the detonation of nuclear warheads in Pakistan and India, and evidence of terrorist groups seeking to acquire nuclear capabilities, there has arguably never been as much pressure on the international community to find solutions to these delicate issues. Currently, there are five nuclear states (China, France, United Kingdom, Russia, and the United States) and three others known to possess nuclear weapons (India, Israel, and Pakistan). Increasingly, the possible acquisition of nuclear weapons by other states and non-state actors makes the threat to international stability and security that much stronger.

So where does this leave the global community in its efforts to stem the tide of WMD proliferation? With the invasion of Iraq initially based on the presumption that WMD existed and then rescinded, the precedent of such presumptuous decision making has suffered tremendously. So how do states that willingly commit to non-proliferation hold accountable those states that do not and what type of negotiations and "carrots" should be offered in order to work toward the full attainment of global security in this realm of weaponry?

The policy brief "Prevention of WMD Proliferation, Globalization, and International Security" by Dr. Vladimir Orlov[1] addresses and responds to exactly these types of questions. He agrees that the implications for WMD policies are some of the most pressing issues to deal with in the security realm in the 21st century. Through a set of case studies (India, Iran, North Korea, Pakistan, and non-state actors), Dr. Orlov analyzes the challenge that the potential proliferation of WMD presents to states, regions, and the international system and what this means for the risk and prevention of proliferation in the near and mid-term future.

Through a detailed yet concise measure of the current global policy issues related to this topic of debate, Dr. Orlov outlines the current nuclear situation in each of his case studies. He then explains that, while international responses have clearly not been sufficient, many options exist for the international community to respond to traditional and non-traditional proliferation threats. It is Dr. Orlov's belief that the only effective responses are those that are both balanced in approach and customized to each of a variety of potential situations.

2. Dilemmas and Our Recommendations

The risk of continued proliferation of WMD worldwide, by states and potentially by non-state actors, brings into question the relevance and future of the non-proliferation architecture and thus presents the international community with a number of policy dilemmas. Most urgently, the international community faces a number of urgent collective decisions concerning potential nuclear states in the area of nuclear non-proliferation. Thus, the table below identifies eight policy dilemmas paired with relevant policy recommendations that aim to increase the confidence of states in multilateral solutions to the proliferation of nuclear weapons and are made in light of warranted concern for increased nuclear proliferation in recent years.

The above dilemmas and recommendations are all important, but only a few of them will be emphasized here, while also highlighting some of the cross-cutting issues. Using a multilateral forum to discuss nuclear proliferation is essential, as is basing action on the international legal instruments available. In this regard, the NPT is the legal cornerstone of the non-proliferation regime, and states rightly put a great deal of emphasis on its central role in encouraging non-proliferation. However, they face increasing pressure to adapt the non-proliferation regime to today's realities: for instance, of eight nuclear states, only five are recognized by the NPT. The NPT remains the bedrock, but other instruments, such as United Nations (UN) Security Council resolutions and ad hoc solutions, must also be instrumentalized.

Second, the determination of certain terrorist organizations to obtain nuclear material poses a grave risk to the world. States face a dilemma in responding to this threat because of the lack of information surrounding who has or is trying to acquire these weapons and the difficulty of detecting storage sites. There need to be tight controls and monitoring to ensure that these weapons do not end up in the wrong hands, including policies that put preventative incentives in place for potential sellers.

Third, the International Atomic Energy Agency (IAEA) and states face policy dilemmas when trying to identify ways to encourage states to give up their nuclear ambitions. Certain potential nuclear states need to be offered important and attractive incentives in order to abandon their military nuclear programs, but these incentives are not always evident. Carrots, as much as sticks, need to be identified. States that are deemed suspicious by the international community still have the right under the nuclear non-proliferation regime to develop nuclear technology for peaceful, domestic purposes, but the international community are not very accepting of "risky states" using their rights to acquire the newest technology for this purpose.

Nuclear states need to offer incentives to maintain or create their nuclear status by ensuring protection, while, to avoid the perception of double standards, they could also reduce their nuclear stockpiles significantly without threatening their own security. Additionally, states should pursue the development of new non-nuclear technology systems. Reducing existing nuclear arsenals would have to be weighed in light of regional security concerns and domestic pressures, but it would be an important confidence-building measure and testament to the importance of the multilateral arrangements under the non-proliferation regime. The trust that states have for one another is of paramount importance in dealing with these issues and quite often it is the first casualty of these discussions.

3. Conclusion

The threat posed by the proliferation of weapons of mass destruction among state and non-state actors looms large over the international community. As some potential nuclear states claim to have a right to conduct nuclear research, countries like the United States find themselves in a difficult negotiating position, being nuclear states themselves. Multilateral solutions must be sought at every turn, and organizations such as the IAEA and the UN must be supported in their nonproliferation endeavors. Specific and collaborative measures will help to further negotiations and the move toward a more secure and stable global society.

References

[1] For the entire policy brief, please see Chapter 6.

CHAPTER 8

THE NON-PROLIFERATION REGIME

SHAHRAM CHUBIN

Dr. Shahram Chubin is Director of Studies and Joint Course Director of the International Training Course in Security Policy at the Geneva Centre for Security Policy, Geneva, Switzerland

Abstract
Changes in international politics and security, energy security, globalization, the emergence of non-state actors, and the diffusion of technology have all put the Nuclear Non-Proliferation Treaty (NPT) under severe strain. As the most adhered to arms-control agreement, the NPT is vulnerable in several respects. First, it was created on the basis of political circumstances that have since changed. Second, it is an unequal treaty and as such is open to criticism. Third, the treaty contains contradictions in simultaneously promoting the use of nuclear technology for providing energy and controlling it for weapons purposes. Since the technology for both purposes is similar, this creates ambiguities and loopholes that can be exploited. Fourth, the treaty has no enforcement mechanism to ensure compliance. If the basic bargain struck in the treaty is to be preserved, a balance will have to found between the rights and responsibilities of all its members, between dealing with individual problem states and the regime as a whole, and in reconciling access to technology for energy purposes but restricting it for weapons purposes. Only such a balance can command the international opinion needed to strengthen the treaty without renegotiating it. Only an integrated approach can preserve the regime while making it more effective in a changed context. The 2005 Review Conference was in Kofi Annan's words a "lost opportunity" in this regard.

1. Policy Challenges

The first set of challenges is related to incentives for nuclear weapons, which appear to have increased.[1] Successfully dealing with the handful of determined proliferators is critical if there is not to be a "cascade" of proliferation.[2]

This assumes at least a consensus in the United Nations (UN) Security Council and preferably a broader consensus on how to move forward and how to enforce compliance. The NPT cannot survive (m)any defections.

Dealing with globalization poses a second set of issues: how to keep nuclear materials out of the hands of terrorist groups in an era of secondary suppliers[3] and dual-use technology that makes limiting and controlling its diffusion more difficult. Dealing with non-state actors is a new challenge for a treaty that assumes state control.

Third, as the demand for nuclear energy as a clean fuel grows, controlling nuclear materials and ensuring their safety will become more difficult.

Fourth, dealing realistically with the three "other" states that are outside the NPT but in fact nuclear (India, Israel, and Pakistan) is important for controlling trade, ensuring safety, and limiting further proliferation.

Fifth, reviving the consensus on the treaty and its basic bargain requires a multilateral approach that balances obligations and rights in an equitable manner. Plugging the gaps in the treaty needs common consent and consultation.

2. Policy Responses

To date, policy responses have been ad hoc and unilateral rather than integrated and enjoying international consensus. The 1995 NPT Review Conference, which barely agreed on an "indefinite extension" of the treaty imparted a false sense of unity for an instrument already fraying. A number of measures worth nothing have been adopted.

The experience of the United Nations Special Commission (UNSCOM) and the United Nations Interim Administration Mission in Kosovo (UNMOVIK) suggest that intrusive inspections can be effective in verifying a program in extreme cases. The Additional Protocol represents a tightening of the original safeguard system, the adoption of which is voluntary and not yet general. The Proliferation Security Initiative (PSI), which is not a treaty-based approach, intended to intercept suspect maritime cargoes, has been adopted by more than 60 states to date. It can act as a deterrent and tighten sanctions that have been approved, but is not formally linked to the NPT. The widespread adoption of, and support for, United Nations Security Council Resolution 1540, making national governments responsible for legislation criminalizing terrorist activity in the area of weapons of mass destruction (WMD) acquisition and reporting to the UN, is a step forward.

In the G8, rather than UN, context, the Cooperative Threat Reduction (CTR) and Global Partnership programs are intended to increase the safety of fissile stocks and materials and personnel with sensitive training that might be put to nefarious purposes.

Other policy responses include those led by the US in relation to North Korea, the 1994 Agreed Framework and current six-party talks, each an attempt to deal with North Korea's motives for proliferation and to dissuade it from this path. International sanctions, US pressure, and the United Kingdom's (UK) role as interlocutor with Libya have been more successful. Tripoli has been encouraged to reverse its policy in exchange for a reduction in its isolation, a case of "policy change" under pressure.

A number of policy responses have been floated but not yet concretized. The director general of the International Atomic Energy Agency (IAEA), Mohamed ElBaradei, has proposed a "moratorium" on new enrichment facilities, an international fuel bank, and assured supplies of fuel. The US and Russia have endorsed this approach.

The US, under the Global Nuclear Energy Partnership (GNEP), has been promoting proliferation-resistant technologies that meet increased energy needs. This remains in the planning stage.[4]

The US has sought to engage India in a strategic partnership, bringing it into some relationship with the Nuclear Suppliers Group (NSG) and according it some of the benefits of joining the NPT. Congress has yet to approve this.

3. Dilemmas

Possible dilemmas stem from likely increased demand for nuclear energy, the problems of technology diffusion attendant to globalization, the need to tighten the treaty without renegotiating it, and the need for consensus that is greater than the lowest common denominator.
 1. How to respond to increased demand for nuclear energy for peaceful purposes without making weapons proliferation easier;

2. How to control technology diffusion without adding to any sense of discrimination;

3. How to reconcile tightening (and enforcing) the treaty with the original "bargain" in the treaty;

4. How to create or restore consensus in a changed context of politics and energy;

5. How to deal effectively with the three-state problem[5] without weakening the principles of the NPT;[6]

6. How to prevent defections from the treaty by dealing with specific cases without "rewarding" potential proliferators; and

7. How to devalue nuclear weapons and their utility for others when the US and France have found new rationales for them.[7]

4. Implications

The difficulty of dealing with the treaty's loopholes, reconstituting consensus between the nuclear- and non-nuclear-weapons states *and* in the Security Council, preventing defections, and dealing with the three major states outside the treaty, without compromising principles, appears formidable.

There is a risk that the NPT, the most important arms-control treaty, will fail. This could come about as a result of several individual or linked events. The NPT regime may simply no longer cover the needs as they exist for technology or security. As a state-based treaty, it may not be able to cover the world of non-state actors. If there are defections, the treaty's function of guaranteeing a non-nuclear world will have been discredited. So will the United Nations Security Council's failure to have met the challenge. The implications of a failure of the most universally adhered to agreement in arms control would surely be to discredit arms control as a whole. It would also result in questioning whether global regimes are feasible in the future. Reconstituting a global regime, a *new* bargain, appears unrealistic, hence the likelihood that the NPT might be followed by regional, zonal, or other more limited approaches. The implications of this is that nuclear material will be less subject to safeguards and controls, that nuclear trafficking will be easier, and that many more governments and terrorist groups will be in a position to exploit the permissive environment to get closer to nuclear weapons.

The implication of unilateral or patchwork responses to a global problem suggests a fragmentation of security. Many areas will have no replacements or substitutes for the NPT. Elsewhere, improvised, non-treaty-based responses will not replace the need for global solutions, however elusive.

5. Trajectories (Scenarios)

There are three or four likely scenarios that could play out in the future.

1. The first is a continuation of the current situation, *muddling through* in a weakened system. Most continue to observe the treaty with all its lacunae and contradictions. No major repairs will be made to the NPT, though there will be some improvisation. There will not be any new consensus or major breakdown. Defections will be limited in number, ambiguous, and contained. The regime will survive because it continues to serve its members' interests, its defects notwithstanding.

    1a) A variant of this is that of *gradual erosion*, a steady unraveling of the treaty, weakening it irreparably. This could come from a failure to address new challenges, revealing that the treaty is shot through with holes. Or it could come from dramatic defections that undermine the treaty's rationale and norms. Few states will adhere to the Additional Protocol, and states will seek nuclear options within the treaty. The NPT will persist through inertia but will be minimally effective and discredited.

2. An alternative is the *sudden collapse* scenario, leading to a free-for-all scramble for nuclear options or weapons. This could stem from a dramatic failure, most probably from a treaty defection by a key state, triggering multiple withdrawals. Alternatively, a failure on the part of the US to meet the perceived security needs of an ally (Taiwan) might see the same result. This "tipping point" could also come from a policy of sustained unilateralism and snubbing of the treaty

provisions by one or more nuclear-weapons states, catalyzing withdrawal by major unsatisfied states. More nuclear-weapons states, official or not, will increase the incentives of others to follow suit. And the emphasis on nuclear weapons, whether for deterrence, blackmail, or offense, will increase.

3. *Regime repaired.* This presupposes a renewal of the treaty and its aims and obligations, a new consensus between the non-nuclear and nuclear-weapons states, as well as within the UN Security Council. This will lead to a strengthened regime that mends its holes in line with the new demands made on it in a changed context. This implies a renewed interest in integrated solutions rooted in a global instrument. This optimum scenario will be the most difficult to achieve. The risks of unregulated or under-regulated commerce in nuclear materials and facilities that have not been safeguarded is self-evident. Whether it is enough to bring about the necessary political will to repair the regime comprehensively is another matter.

6. Recommendations

The key threats to the NPT are still limited to a few states; how they are dealt with will affect the treaty's future. So far, there have not been any cases of nuclear terrorism, though all governments have sufficient incentive to take this issue seriously (see UN Security Council Resolution 1540). Even the most intrusive inspections are of limited effectiveness. Technology denial has limits and needs global cooperation. Renegotiation of the treaty is impracticable, but its revival needs general consensus. Nuclear non-proliferation is a "collective public good"[8] that needs a sustained and expanded foundation of political support for its goals.

1. Reduce reliance on nuclear weapons, eliminate tactical nuclear weapons, extend security assurances (positive and negative) to non-nuclear-weapons states and seek limits among new nuclear states (India, Israel, and Pakistan);

2. Make adoption of the Additional Protocol mandatory for problem states and preferably for all states;

3. Provide more resources for inspections and verification. Change the rationale/attitude behind inspections from examining declared sites to *investigating* any suspicions of weapons diversion;

4. Make withdrawal from the NPT more difficult (Art. X) and, in any case, subject to penalties in which the withdrawing state is unable to benefit from access to technology gained while in the treaty;[9]

5. Strengthen the UN Security Council's role in enforcing compliance with the NPT. The Security Council could oblige non-compliant states to accept tougher inspections and give up sensitive technologies for a given period of time;[10]

6. Dealing with the other, or three-state, problem should focus on bringing these states into the NSG in order to strengthen the mechanisms controlling trade in nuclear materials;

7. Bring unilateral or other initiatives into line with Global Partnership in nuclear issues;

8. Encourage proliferation technologies and dependence on alternative fuels;

9. Adopt a five- to ten-year moratorium on new enrichment facilities (especially among states that do not yet possess enrichment) in line with ElBaradei's various proposals; and

10. Internationalize the nuclear-fuel cycle. Guarantee the supply of reactor technology/nuclear fuel. Create a framework for the multilateral management of the "back end" of the fuel cycle (spent fuel and reprocessing) and the front end (enrichment, fuel production).

The list of suggestions outstrips available support. For the foreseeable future, the likely scenario is one of muddling through with, over time, erosion for support for the treaty/regime. In the case of dramatic failure or defections, this process will be accelerated, leading to the scenario of complete collapse, with its attendant consequences.

References

[1] Speaking before the Senate Select Committee on February 11, 2003, CIA Director G. Tenet said that "The desire for nuclear weapons is on the increase." In February 2006, US Ambassador John Negroponte, Director of National Intelligence, noted that 40 countries were seeking dual-use WMD. An analyst has suggested that the balance between disincentives and incentives for seeking nuclear weapons may have changed today. See M. Reiss, "The Nuclear Tipping Point: Prospects for a World of Many Nuclear Weapons States," in K. Campbell, R. Einhorn, M. Reiss, *The Nuclear Tipping Point: Why States Reconsider Their Nuclear Choices* (Washington, DC: The Brookings Institute, 2004), pp. 12-13.

[2] In the words of the UN High Level Panel, which saw the NPT as close to the point of "irreversible" erosion.

[3] Such as A.Q. Khan's network or Malaysia.

[4] "Bush Promotes New Nuclear Plan," *Arms Control Today*, March 2006, pp. 16-17.

[5] The OS or three-state problem refers to the three non-signatories to the NPT (India, Israel, and Pakistan) that have nuclear weapons but, being outside the treaty, are not formally recognized as nuclear-weapons states (NWS) and are outside the nuclear suppliers group (NSG) as well.

[6] The *Financial Times* called the proposed US-Indian Civil Nuclear Agreement of July 2005 an effort to cooperate with India to bring some of that state's facilities under safeguards as "a terrible precedent against everything the NPT stands for." Pakistan's foreign minister predicted that it would destroy the NPT, *Financial Times*, March 17, 2006, p. 6.

[7] The US versus other WMD and as possible "bunker busters" and the French against terrorists. See "Chirac Outlines Expanded Nuclear Doctrine," *Arms Control Today*, March 2006, pp. 43-44.

[8] See E. Asculai, "Rethinking the Nuclear Non-Proliferation Regime," Jaffee Centre, Memorandum 70, June 2004.

[9] The French government has suggested this.

[10] Suggestions on these lines have been made by Pierre Goldschmidt, formerly of the IAEA. A brief reference is found in "A rare diplomatic unity," *The Economist*, February 4, 2006, p. 11. A more extended version can be found on the Carnegie Endowment website, see http://www.carnegieendowment.org/.

CHAPTER 9

EDITORIAL OF POLICY BRIEF ON THE
NON-PROLIFERATION REGIME

NAYEF R.F. AL-RODHAN

Dr. Nayef R.F. Al-Rodhan is Senior Scholar in Geostrategy and Director of the Program on the Geopolitical Implications of Globalization and Transnational Security at the Geneva Centre for Security Policy, Geneva, Switzerland

1. Review and Critique

As Robert Jervis once stated, "[a] rational strategy for the employment of nuclear weapons is a contradiction in terms," since their destructive power creates impenetrable problems.[1] Following a considerable degree of pessimism in the 1980s about the prospects of a possible nuclear war, the 1990s were characterized by a great deal of hope about the diminishing relevance of nuclear weapons. Yet, against the hopes of many, the end of the bipolar system did not signal a decline in the relevance of nuclear weapons. The former superpowers continue to hold a large number of strategic, as well as tactical, nuclear weapons. China has modernized its nuclear arsenal. A number of new nuclear-weapons states (NWS) have appeared (India, Israel, and Pakistan) since the Nuclear Non-Proliferation Treaty (NPT) was established in 1968. And Iran and North Korea may soon join the nuclear club. Thus, the possibility of nuclear-weapons proliferation destabilizing various regions is very real.

One of the major problems afflicting the NPT is the fundamental contradiction at its heart: It banned the possession and control of nuclear weapons for all states except the original five NWS – the United States, Russia/Soviet Union, the United Kingdom, France, and China. Non-nuclear-weapons states (NNWS) that signed on to the NPT agreed not to acquire or develop nuclear weapons in the expectation that NWS would work toward nuclear-weapons disarmament. Yet, this has failed to transpire. Thus, the NPT rings hollow to many NNWS that agreed to restrict their own military buildup in the expectation that NWS would continue to work toward disarmament.[2]

Moreover, with the end of the Cold War, there is no longer a clear consensus on how best to ensure global security and stability. This makes progress in the area of nuclear non-proliferation extremely difficult to achieve. As Shahram Chubin notes in his policy brief, how best to restore consensus in a changed security and energy context poses a considerable challenge to the nuclear non-proliferation regime. For example, how can the non-proliferation regime respond to the demand for nuclear energy as a "clean" fuel and, at the same time, control the spread of nuclear materials and guarantee their safety? And how can it successfully deal with India, Israel, and Pakistan without encouraging other states to "go nuclear?"[3]

An additional challenge to the NPT is also identified by Chubin. The nuclear non-proliferation regime faces the problem of preventing nuclear materials from falling into terrorist hands, given the existence of secondary suppliers and dual-use technology. Indeed, dealing with non-state actors represents a new problem for the NPT. As a state-based treaty, the NPT may not be able to adequately ensure nuclear non-proliferation in an environment in which non-state actors play an increasingly important role.

2. Dilemmas and Our Recommendations

Globalization, therefore, presents a series of serious challenges for the NPT. How to respond to them, however, remains highly contested. Reaching a consensus on how to deal with the problems facing the NPT will be vital to confirming its continued relevance, as well as ensuring its effectiveness. In what follows, we highlight eight dilemmas related to this issue and eight corresponding recommendations that may contribute to appropriate policy choices.

As alluded to earlier, one of the major challenges facing the NPT is the difficulty of controlling dual-use technology. The NPT allows states to develop nuclear energy but prevents the development of nuclear weapons. Yet, the technology required to reach both ends is similar. In order to overcome this hurdle, proliferation-resistant technology that can only be used for the production of energy should be developed. An additional difficulty is posed by the supply of dual-

use technology by non-state secondary actors. Monitoring and controlling the supply of such technology by these actors is particularly difficult given that the NPT is a state-based treaty. We suggest that multilateral security cooperation should be encouraged. Preventive maritime inspections of the Proliferation Security Initiative (PSI), for instance, should also be strengthened and possibly linked to the NPT in some way.

Members of the NPT face the additional problem of effectively dealing with the three nuclear states that remain outside the Treaty. Yet, they need to do so without appearing to be hypocritical and discriminatory in preventing further proliferation. In particular, it is essential to avoid the perception that challenging the NPT will be rewarded by cooperation.

Responding appropriately to these new nuclear-weapons powers is vital to ameliorating regional instabilities and, in the worst-case scenario, avoiding nuclear exchanges. Given the fragility of Indian-Pakistani relations, as well as volatility in the Middle East, a broader effort should also be made to reduce underlying tensions within these regions. Specifically, outstanding conflicts should be resolved in order to lessen the perceived need for nuclear deterrence. Multilateral alliances should also be encouraged in order to prevent blackmail or aggressive regional strategies.

The NPT will also have to find a way of reconciling increased global energy demands, the need to employ "clean" and durable energy, and the proliferation of technologies and materials that may be used to develop nuclear weapons. In order to achieve these seemingly contradictory ends, a number of measures should be taken. First, the International Atomic Energy Agency (IAEA) should be expanded. Second, an international fuel bank should be established as a reliable source of nuclear fuel. It is important to stress, however, that such a bank should be subjected to stringent inspections aimed at monitoring its energy use.

3. Conclusion

While the NPT has failed to prevent states from developing nuclear weapons, it is the best we have at the moment. Yet, the challenges facing the NPT in a changed security and energy environment are daunting. Perhaps the biggest problem facing the non-proliferation regime is the lack of consensus on how best to respond to threats to security and stability. Another major obstacle to preventing nuclear proliferation is the nature of the NPT itself. Since it is state-based, it is confronted with the challenge of responding to non-state proliferators. Moreover, increased demand for nuclear energy makes the task of controlling the spread of nuclear weapons even more difficult due to the dual usage of the technology required for nuclear-energy and nuclear-weapons programs.

References

[1] R. Jervis, *The Illogic of American Nuclear Strategy* (Ithaca and London: Cornell University Press, 1984), p. 19.

[2] See J. Krause and A. Wenger (eds.), *Nuclear Weapons into the 21st Century: Current Trends and Future Prospects* (Bern, etc.: Peter Lang, 2001).

[3] For the brief in its entirety, please see Chapter 8.

CHAPTER 10

PROLIFERATION, NON-STATE ACTORS, AND THE
IMPACT ON GLOBAL SECURITY

WAHEGURU PAL SINGH SIDHU

Dr. Waheguru Pal Singh Sidhu is Course Director of the New Issues in Security Course at the Geneva Centre for Security Policy, Geneva, Switzerland

Abstract
Nuclear proliferation by non-state actors poses three challenges for global security: first, defining non-state actors; second, preventing the acquisition of nuclear arms and material by non-state actors; and, third, preventing their use and, in a worst-case scenario, dealing with the consequences of the use of these weapons. In responses to these challenges, the international community has grappled, unsuccessfully, with defining non-state actors and has had limited success in strengthening the capacity of states to prevent proliferation. However, the international community is at least prepared to deal with the use or the threat of use of these weapons by non-state actors. Consequently, in the foreseeable future, non-state actors will continue to proliferate, as the present set of proliferation tools are likely to remain inadequate. Hence, there will be a greater impetus to develop ad hoc, short-term, unilateral or multilateral responses to addressing the immediate challenges posed by proliferation among non-state actors. In turn, these ad hoc responses might further weaken the existing treaty-based non-proliferation regime. Therefore, in the long run the existing non-proliferation regime will have to be revamped in a significant way to address the old (state-centered) and new (non-state-centered) challenges. Among the recommendations for achieving this goal are: banning the possession and outlawing the use of nuclear weapons by all states, including the original five nuclear-weapons states (in the long run); strengthening the capacity of states to deal with non-state actors (in the medium term); and, only in the most exceptional case, using military action to prevent such proliferation (in the short term). However, such military action should be based on extremely accurate intelligence and the consensus of the international community.

1. Policy Challenges

Nuclear proliferation by non-state actors poses the latest and, perhaps, the most formidable challenge to global security and to the already beleaguered nuclear non-proliferation regime.[1]

The first policy challenge is to define non-state actors. According to United Nations (UN) Security Council Resolution 1540 of April 28, 2004, a non-state actor is an "individual or entity, not acting under the lawful authority of any State." This broad definition is relevant for most instances but does not cover all contingencies. For instance, if the laws of a state do not explicitly ban proliferation, then can an individual or entity that indulges in proliferation activities be considered a non-state actor? Moreover, while the definition focuses on individuals and entities, it does not take into consideration the existence of a failed state or a state which might itself indulge in proliferation.

The second policy challenge is to prevent the acquisition of nuclear arms and material by non-state actors, however defined. Although non-state actors have in the past acquired and used both chemical and biological weapons, these actors and capabilities have been almost exclusively homegrown.[2] In contrast, there is a general perception that acquisition of nuclear arms and material would require some degree of transnational cooperation among states and non-state actors and could not be entirely homegrown. The exception would be a state possessing nuclear weapons that fails and becomes a non-state with nuclear weapons or that some non-state actor in that failed state acquires its nuclear weapons.

The third policy challenge is to prevent the use of nuclear weapons once they have been acquired by non-state actors and, in a worst-case scenario, to deal with the consequences of the deliberate or accidental use of these terrible weapons. While deterrence theory has largely been credited with preventing the use of nuclear weapons among states, it is not clear that deterrence would be equally effective in preventing the use of nuclear weapons by non-state actors.

2. Responses

In response to the first challenge, the international community has sought to distinguish, however imperfectly, between states and non-state actors and to restrict the illegal activities of the latter through the former.

In response to the second challenge, the international community has sought to strengthen the capacity of states through a series of ad hoc carrot-and-stick initiatives, although there has been greater emphasis on sticks. Among the carrots are the G-8 Global Partnership, which is aimed primarily at preventing the exodus of nuclear material and expertise from the former Soviet Union, as well as other nuclear states. A related incentive is evident in UN Security Council Resolution 1540, which calls on states to pass legislation to "prohibit any non-State actor to manufacture, acquire, possess, develop, transport, transfer or use nuclear, chemical or biological weapons and their means of delivery" and implicitly offers to assist states in drafting such laws.[3] Among the sticks are a series of export-control measures aimed at preventing the acquisition of nuclear material and technology by non-nuclear states that are perceived to be proliferation risks. Perhaps the biggest stick in this respect is the Proliferation Security Initiative (PSI) launched by the United States (US) and a handful of like-minded nations to interdict suspected shipments of nuclear components through their territories. Although aimed at states rather than non-state actors, the incentive is also likely to impact on the activities of non-state actors.[4]

However, the international response to the third challenge has been the weakest. In the first instance, no one, the recent statement by French President Jacques Chirac notwithstanding, has seriously considered the relevance (or irrelevance) of deterring the potential nuclear weapons of non-state actors with nuclear weapons of states.[5] Although countries like the US have clearly planned for pre-emptive strikes (under the present administration) against potential nuclear threats by non-state actors, operationalizing such a strategy would depend on the ability to provide a higher level of intelligence than has been available until now.

However, no state has seriously contemplated possible responses in the case that a non-state actor acquired a nuclear weapon and none is prepared for such an eventuality. Even today, as UN Secretary General Kofi Annan has noted, "a nuclear catastrophe in one of our great cities" would only raise questions ranging from whether it was a terrorist act or aggression by a state or an accident. While these scenarios "may not be equally probable, but all are possible,"[6] no response has been prepared.

3. Dilemmas

There are a series of dilemmas that are hindering current responses. The first is the continued relevance of nuclear weapons among nuclear- and non-nuclear-weapons states for global security. This means that those states that depend on nuclear weapons for their own security have the unenviable task of trying to deny others the same right. In contrast with biological and chemical weapons, which have been banned for everyone, thereby making it easy to justify banning them even for non-state actors, no similar justification is possible for non-state actors seeking nuclear weapons. This has led to a curious and dangerous relationship between some states and some non-state actors seeking nuclear weapons.[7]

Second, as the existing non-proliferation regime was designed to deal with states, they are ill-equipped to address non-state actors. Consequently, on account of the perceived urgency of the threat posed by non-state actors, many states, particularly the United States, have embarked on a series of ad hoc responses that, while apparently strong on action, are weak in law. This has created a dilemma of legitimacy regarding some of these measures, especially as they focus more on sticks than carrots.

Third, there is the dilemma of "second-tier nuclear proliferation" or "secondary proliferation,"[8] facilitated by the globalization of manufacturing capabilities, which allows companies even in non-nuclear states, such as Malaysia, to develop vital components to build nuclear weapons. Consequently non-state actors today have greater access to vital nuclear technology.[9] This simply means that, in an increasingly globalized world, focusing on states alone is unlikely to be sufficient; it is also essential to engage private manufacturers.

4. Implications

Today, thanks to the initial set of responses to prevent nuclear proliferation by non-state actors, there are three sets of regimes in existence. First, there is the multilateral institutional non-proliferation regime anchored in negotiated treaties, such as the Nuclear Non-Proliferation Treaty (NPT) and the Comprehensive Test Ban Treaty (CTBT) These treaties invariably tend to be weak on enforcement but strong in law, e.g., the NPT is as incapable of enforcing Article X (withdrawal from the treaty) as it is Article VI (nuclear disarmament).[10]

Second, there is the multilateral non-treaty-based regime, established by various declarations and resolutions made by the UN Security Council and the UN General Assembly. In the case of the Security Council, these include Resolutions 1373 and 1540.[11] In the case of the General Assembly, this includes the resolution related to the CTBT, as well the more recent International Convention for the Suppression of Acts of Nuclear Terrorism. This regime provides a helpful stopgap arrangement to plug existing loopholes and also salvage treaties that might otherwise have ended in dustbins. However, there is concern that this approach, especially if exercised often enough by the Security Council, would circumvent the negotiated approach to developing treaty-based regimes.

Third, there is an emerging ad hoc, non-institutional, non-conventional regime based on initiatives, such as the PSI, the European Union (EU) 3's negotiations with Iran, and the six-party talks to address the challenge posed by North Korea's nuclear ambitions. This ad hoc regime tends to be stronger on the enforcement dimension but is relatively weak in law. There is also concern that there is no sunset clause for these ad hoc arrangements.

The primary implication of the presence of these three regimes is that they are not necessarily complementary but might, in fact, be divisive and competitive, especially as no effort has been made to harmonize the three. Indeed, there is a distinct possibility that the ad hoc initiatives by both the UN Security Council and groups of countries might actually weaken the already stressed treaty-based non-proliferation regime even further.

5. Future Trajectories/Scenarios

First, in the foreseeable future, non-state actors will continue to play an important part in proliferation and, therefore, also have an impact on international peace and security. Second, the present set of proliferation tools, especially the state-centric, treaty-based non-proliferation regime, is likely to remain inadequate to address the challenge posed by non-state actors. Third, consequently, there will be a greater impetus to develop ad hoc, short-term, unilateral or multilateral responses to addressing the immediate challenges posed by proliferation among non-state actors. Fourth, in the wake of this ad hoc trend, which seeks short-term and immediate solutions, there is grave danger that the treaty-based non-proliferation regime might be inadvertently further weakened. This was apparent in the 2005 NPT Review Conference. One reason for the failure of the conference was that there were no deals to be made within the NPT setting (as was the case at the 1995 and 2000 Review Conferences). All of the action was happening outside the General Assembly hall. Finally, actors will continue to make efforts to try to bridge the gap between the three pillars – the treaty-based regime, the non-treaty-based multilateral regime, and the ad hoc, non-institutional regime – by seeking to legitimize the ad hoc initiatives and also to link them to existing treaty-based regimes. This has been sought through endorsements by the UN General Assembly and the Security Council, efforts at universalization, and simply by being more effective. However, these efforts have limited appeal and scope. In the long run, the existing non-proliferation regime will have to be revamped in a significant way to address the old (state-centered) and new (non-state-centered) challenges.

6. Policy Recommendations

1. In the long term, to create a world order not based on the possession of nuclear weapons, it would be vital to outlaw and eventually ban nuclear weapons (as has already been done in the case of biological and chemical weapons). This would make possession by anyone, including the five original nuclear-weapons states – the United States, the Russian Federation, the United Kingdom, France, and China – and the three other nuclear-weapons states – India, Israel, and Pakistan – as well as non-state actors illegal and would require a nuclear-weapons convention similar to the biological- and chemical-weapons convention.[12]

2. In the medium term, the international community should take steps to strengthen and enhance the capacity of states to prevent the proliferation of nuclear weapons among non-state actors within their borders by providing them with necessary incentives

and tools for doing so. In this context, UN Security Council Resolution 1540 is a good start, although its incentive side should be enhanced.

3. While strengthening the capacity of states to counter the challenges posed by non-state actors seeking nuclear weapons, care should be taken to ensure that the existing treaty-based non-proliferation regime is given center stage and strengthened.[13]

4. In addition, countries of particular concern as potential suppliers for non-state actors, as well as the target of non-state nuclear suppliers, should be engaged with a new series of incentives to dismantle existing nuclear networks and prevent the emergence of new ones.[14]

5. In the short term, a series of sticks, short of military action, might also be considered to raise the stakes for non-state actors seeking to either acquire or supply nuclear weapons. Such sticks could be a combination of smart sanctions, increased vigilance, and police action related to the illegal movement of nuclear material and technology.

6. In the short term, and only in the most extreme case, should military action against non-state actors be considered. However, such action would require not only a higher level of accurate intelligence but also the consensus of the international community. Otherwise, such action is likely to backfire with even more dire consequences.

References

[1] The nuclear non-proliferation regime consists of the Partial Test Ban Treaty (1963), the Nuclear Non-Proliferation Treaty (1970), the Convention on the Physical Protection of Nuclear Material (1987), the Comprehensive Test Ban Treaty (1996), the various Nuclear-Weapon-Free Zones, as well as the various supply-control regimes, such as the Nuclear Suppliers Group (1975). This regime is already facing challenges from states that are within and outside the regime.

[2] Both the Biological Weapons Convention and the Chemical Weapons Convention (as well as their implementing agency, the Organization for the Prohibition of Chemical Weapons) have banned the possession and use of biological and chemical weapons, which is not the case with nuclear weapons.

[3] See UN Security Council Resolution 1540 of April 28, 2004, S/RES/1540 (2004).

[4] This was evident in the case of the interception of the German-owned "BBC China," which was carrying centrifuge parts to Libya built in Malaysia and shipped via Dubai for the Dr. A.Q. Khan network. For details of the PSI, see S.A. Squassoni, S.R. Bowman, and C.E. Behrens, "Proliferation Control Regimes: Background and Status," CRS Report for Congress, February 10, 2005, p. 15; for details of the "BBC China" interception, see D. Albright and C. Hinderstein, "Unraveling the A.Q. Khan and Future Proliferation Networks," *The Washington Quarterly*, Spring 2005, pp. 111-128.

[5] French President Jacques Chirac is the only one who publicly but tentatively raised the possibility of deterring non-state actors with nuclear weapons. See the speech by Jacques Chirac during his visit to the Strategic Air and Maritime Forces at Landivisiau/L'Ile Longue, Brest (Finistère), January 19, 2006, available at http://www.elysee.fr/elysee/elysee.fr/anglais/speeches_and_documents/2006/speech_by_jacques_chirac_president_of_the_french_republic_during_his_visit_to_the_stategic_forces.38447.html; A. MacLachlan and M. Hibbs, "Chirac shifts French doctrine for use of nuclear weapons," *Nucleonics Week*, January 26, 2006.

[6] United Nations Secretary-General Kofi Annan's address to the Nuclear Non-Proliferation Treaty Review Conference, New York, May 2, 2005, Press Release, SG/SM/9847DC/2956.

[7] This is most evident in the case of the A.Q. Khan network, which, apart from supplying sensitive nuclear material and designs to Iran, Libya, and North Korea, is also suspected of having links with armed non-state groups. The motivations for dealing with the latter include the presence of nuclear-weapons states, as well as the perceived anti-Muslim policies of some of these states.

[8] See C. Braun and C.F. Chayba, "Proliferation Rings," *International Security*, Vol. 29, No. 2, Fall 2004, pp. 5-6 for "second-tier nuclear proliferation," which has been defined as when "states in the developing world with varying technical capabilities trade among themselves to bolster one another's nuclear and strategic weapons efforts"; see C. Clary, "Dr. Khan's Nuclear Walmart," *Disarmament Diplomacy*, No. 76, March/April 2004, for "secondary proliferation" and "globalization of manufacturing."

[9] For details, see Albright and Hinderstein, *op. cit.* note 4.

[10] For further information see http://www.un.org/Depts/dda/WMD/treaty/.

[11] Please see United Nations Security Council Resolution 1373 of September 28, 2001, available at http://daccessdds.un.org/doc/UNDOC/GEN/N01/557/43/PDF/N0155743.pdf?OpenElement; United Nations Security Council Resolution 1540 of April 28, 2004, available at http://daccessdds.un.org/doc/UNDOC/GEN/N04/328/43/PDF/N0432843.pdf?OpenElement.

[12] See http://www.ippnw.org/NWC.html for details of the model Nuclear Weapons Convention.

[13] See H. Müller, "Reviving the Disarmament Regimes: Recommendations of the High Level Panel and the Secretary General's Advisory Board," *Disarmament Diplomacy*, No. 80, Autumn 2005.

[14] For details, please see A.H. Montgomery, "Ringing in Proliferation," *International Security*, Vol. 30, No. 2, Fall 2005, pp. 179-187.

CHAPTER 11

EDITORIAL OF POLICY BRIEF ON PROLIFERATION, NON-STATE ACTORS, AND THE IMPACT ON GLOBAL SECURITY

NAYEF R.F. AL-RODHAN

Dr. Nayef R.F. Al-Rodhan is Senior Scholar in Geostrategy and Director of the Program on the Geopolitical Implications of Globalization and Transnational Security at the Geneva Centre for Security Policy, Geneva, Switzerland

1. Review and Critique

Following the end of the Cold War, there was a considerable degree of optimism with regard to the diminishing relevance of nuclear weapons. Yet, rather than being marginalized, nuclear weapons continue to be perceived by some as essential to responding to today's challenges to security and stability. At the heart of the nuclear-arms-control (and, thus, non-proliferation) crisis is what Joachim Krause has dubbed "nuclear orthodoxy."[1] Major nuclear powers have sought to preserve as far as possible their old nuclear postures, establishments, and weaponry. Large numbers of strategic, as well as tactical, nuclear weapons are still held by the former superpowers, and China has modernized its nuclear arsenal.

The Nuclear Non-Proliferation Treaty (NPT) is plagued by the inconsistency which provides a fundamental core of its power. The possession and control of nuclear weapons was banned for some, but not the accepted nuclear powers (the United States, Russia/Soviet Union, the United Kingdom, France, and China) under the auspicious that these states would work towards disarming their nuclear arsenals. Due to the fact that this has failed to materialize, the NPT has lost much of its credibility.[2] Additionally, since the establishment of the NPT, a number of other de facto nuclear states have emerged (India, Israel, and Pakistan) and there are other states which are working towards this status as well (Iran and North Korea). Subsequently, regional stability faces a prominent threat through the proliferation and possession of nuclear weapons.

As Brad Roberts notes, there are also states that are determined to gain the strategic leverage that possession of weapons of mass destruction is presumed to bring. The motivation for proliferation has also changed. What drove proliferation in the 1950s and 1960s is not what propels proliferation today: in many cases, regional competition.[3]

As Waheguru Pal Singh Sidhu notes in his policy brief, preventing non-state actors from acquiring nuclear arms and materials poses an additional challenge.[4] The nuclear non-proliferation regime faces the problem of preventing terrorist groups from acquiring nuclear materials. This task is made especially difficult given the existence of secondary suppliers and dual-use technology. Indeed, dealing with non-state actors represents a new problem for the state-based NPT as non-state actors continually increase their influence. Yet, this also means that there will be a greater impetus to develop ad hoc, short-term, unilateral responses to address proliferation by non-state actors. Such actions risk further weakening the existing treaty-based non-proliferation regime.

Thus, while the Cold War rivalry has disappeared, the much anticipated "new world order" has failed to appear. Failure to address persistent security concerns has, as Mohamed ElBaradei has lamented, resulted in a "new world instability."[5] The non-proliferation regime has now to prevent not only states from proliferating but also non-state actors that fall outside of multilateral measures. Thus, the non-proliferation regime will need to be overhauled in order to deal more effectively not only with states but also with non-state proliferators.

2. Dilemmas and Our Recommendations

At present, no consensus exists as to how best to respond to the above-mentioned challenges. The understanding of how the non-proliferation regime can be effective and relevant will be the key to resolving many of the threats surrounding proliferation. We identify eight dilemmas related to this issue area and eight corresponding recommendations that may contribute to the debate.

The non-proliferation regime faces serious challenges as a result of non-state proliferators. A large part of the long-term solution to this problem lies with nuclear states. A reduction of the proliferation threat posed by non-state actors requires at least the eventual marginalization of nuclear weapons by nuclear powers themselves – that means the P5, as well as three new nuclear states currently outside the NPT. This presents a formidable challenge, given the continued "nuclear orthodoxy" shared by the P5, not to mention the fact that additional states are "determined proliferators" and are motivated by a variety of factors.

New supplier nations also render the task of preventing non-state proliferators all the more complex, given the diffusion of materials, technologies, and expertise that have both civilian and military uses, as well as their position outside the NPT.[6] As ElBaradei has pointed out, the current system of export controls is also inadequate in that it relies on informal arrangements that are non-binding, limited in membership, and, moreover, that fail to include many countries with growing industrial capacities.[7]

The necessary response to non-state actors that are suspected of having gained nuclear capacity is also complex. Should states, for example, engage in ad hoc, unilateral, punitive actions? In our view, all ad hoc responses should be avoided, since they undermine multilateral efforts to control the spread of nuclear weapons. Instead, coordinated and multilateral policies should be encouraged. One of the difficulties that must be faced when taking any form of punitive action is that of ascertaining whether proliferation has, in fact, taken place. Inaccurate assessments may only help to nurture the perception that hidden geopolitical motives are at play. Thus, it is imperative that intelligence be developed through the use of multiple sources, as well as through a considerable degree of intelligence sharing between countries. In addition, multilateral approaches, based on information and intelligence cooperation, ought to be backed up by United Nations mandates in order to lend legitimacy to non-proliferation measures.

Responding to non-state proliferators also raises another issue: How should non-state proliferators that are political groups in conflict areas be dealt with? Ultimately, a lasting solution to the problem depends on addressing the root causes of insecurity and instability, which include both regional rivalries and conflicts.[8] Resolution of all conflicts should be sought in order to undermine the true motivation of non-state proliferators that obtain nuclear materials either for their own survival or as instruments of other states. The effectiveness of responses also depends on being able to make the distinction between non-state proliferators that act as appendages of states and non-state organizations that act independently from states.

3. Conclusion

Perhaps the lack of consensus on how best to respond to threats to security and stability is one of the biggest obstacles to progress in the area of non-proliferation. Non-state proliferators provide a challenge to states, primarily because they are extremely difficult to deal with through traditional non-proliferation measures. Over the long term, ongoing regional competition and conflicts, as well as the gap between rich and poor, should be ameliorated. In the short to medium term, multilateral efforts to prevent, as well as to deal with, proliferation should be strengthened.

References

[1] J. Krause, "The Crisis in Nuclear Arms Control," in J. Krause and A. Wenger (eds.), *Nuclear Weapons into the 21st Century: Current Trends and Future Prospects* (Bern, etc.: Peter Lang, 2001), p. 26.
[2] Krause and Wenger, *ibid.*
[3] B. Roberts, "Rethinking N + 1," *National Interest*, No. 51, Spring 1998.
[4] For the brief in its entirety, please see Chapter 10.
[5] M. ElBaradei, "Nuclear Non-proliferation: Global Security in a Rapidly Changing World," Statements of the Director, Washington, DC, June 21, 2004.
[6] *Ibid.*
[7] *Ibid.*
[8] *Ibid.*

CHAPTER 12

ARMS CONTROL IN A GLOBALIZED WORLD

PÁL DUNAY

Dr. Pál Dunay is the former Director of the International Training Course in Security Policy at the Geneva Centre for Security Policy, Geneva, Switzerland and Senior Researcher at the Stockholm International Peace Research Institute, Stockholm, Sweden

Abstract
Arms control has been a less visible component of international affairs since the end of the Cold War and has no chance to return to center stage of world politics. This does not mean an irrevocable crisis of arms control but rather a redefinition of its role. The new areas of arms control that emerge nowadays are far less symbolic than some of their predecessors were at a time when the limitation of armaments was often confined to areas and systems that no party wanted to deploy/employ anyway. The new dimensions of arms control are linked either to the concept of human security or to development policy or both. The arms-control community collides with the community of humanitarians or those of development economics, and hence the course of development of arms control is less predictable than in the past. Considerations other than those of the arms-control community have a major impact on the course of its future evolution. The broadening of the arms-control agenda prevents it, on the one hand, from receding into oblivion. On the other hand, however, it creates blurred boundaries that result in confusion.

Non-proliferation has gained autonomy from the once existent body of arms control and hence it is no longer integrated in it. Consequently, arms control "redux" (arms control without non-proliferation measures) does not receive the same amount of attention it once did. There are two options in front of arms control: either to integrate those arms-control-like activities and arrangements that have gained relevance or to continue to define arms control narrowly and live with its loss of relevance, at least in relative terms.

1. Policy Challenges

Systemic challenges and the unipolar system of international security

1. The international system has been unipolar since the end of the Cold War. This unipolarity is clearest in terms of international security or, even more narrowly defined, in terms of military security, where United States (US) power is preponderant.

2. As the United States is the only global power in international security, security issues are ranked on an international basis in terms of US priorities. This ranking is not completely arbitrary, however, as it is determined by objective reality, at least to some extent. Furthermore, the unipolar power is a democracy that curtails its freedom of action, the role of the legislative and public opinion being good examples. Conflicts gain international relevance based upon rankings in both of these groups. Unless the United States is determined to address an international conflict, it is unlikely to be given much international attention or be treated with much urgency.

3. The US has a variety of means at its disposal to influence international security. From its point of view, there are a variety of means that are more effective at influencing security postures than arms control is. Arms control, in the broad sense, does play a role for the US in terms of proliferation. This involves a set of measures primarily to retain the dominance of legitimate nuclear powers vis-à-vis emerging ones, as well as measures related to humanitarian arms control. The latter helps maintain the image of the US as a liberal power and not one that bases its decisions on power realism. Except for these measures, arms control is of secondary importance in shaping international security.

4. Whereas the above phenomenon is, objectively, of lasting relevance, the legal nihilism of the current US administration is based on the subjective impressions of the current US leadership and may not outlive it.[1]

5. If the assumption that bipolarity results in fewer conflict dyads than multipolarity were correct, then unipolarity would result in even fewer conflict dyads and could be optimal to guarantee international stability. As this assumption cannot be proven, the conclusion can be drawn that unipolarity is a favorable security system for those counties that do not have a competing agenda with the unipolar power or that do not confront it otherwise.

6. For a world that is globalized primarily in technological, economic, and cultural terms, it is difficult to cope with international security that carries an overwhelmingly regional legacy, except for proliferation-type measures (the Nuclear Non-Proliferation Treaty (NPT), the Biological Weapons Convention (BWC), the Chemical Weapons Convention (CWC), supplier groups, the Proliferation Security Initiative (PSI)). Other arms-control measures, largely developed in Europe, have the prospect of being utilized/copied elsewhere. The introduction of parallel measures in other regions may result in some similarity (parallelism) of the arms-control *acquis* in the world but not in its globalization.

7. Currently, non-state actors have gained center stage in terms of international security. They are the main sources of concern and hence it is their behavior that should be influenced in order to change the security situation. It is impossible to imagine using arms-control in relation to terrorist groups, for example. As interstate relations are not the center of international security, arms-control measures cannot address the most important security concern.[2]

The geographical shift in international security and the decline of arms control

8. Since the end of the Cold War, Europe has lost its place at the center of military confrontation and has gradually become a continent of peace where the political agenda is dominated by matters other than security. Europe was not only the center of military confrontation but that of arms control as well. This move thus means leaving the region where the arms-control

acquis has been the richest. It was in the sense that arms control was conditional of a conflict since it emerged as a direct result thereof. Arms control was conditional of the widely familiar destructive capacity of weapons invented during World War II including nuclear weapons but also cruise missiles. Although the East-West conflict of the Cold War era was not an armed conflict *per se*, it often gave the impression it was.

9. In regions outside of the Euro-Atlantic area, arms control has been largely confined to participation in global arms-control measures. Although some arms-control measures have appeared (like confidence-building in the border zones of Central Asia), they are still rudimentary and of marginal importance. Hence, there is no reason to expect that arms control in other regions will provide inertia for the "renaissance" of arms control generally.

2. Responses

When the Cold War ended, it left in place a body of arms-control arrangements, both in the Soviet-American and the European contexts, as well as establishments dealing with such matters. The former was a legacy that had to be addressed to decide on its continuation and eventual adaptation. The latter was a large group of people who had a vested interest in the process.

The arguments put forward since the end of the East-West conflict can be grouped as follows:

1. It was emphasized in the beginning of the 1990s that the process of arms control had not come to an end with the conclusion of agreements, it includes their implementation, verification and operating those forums established in relation to them (e.g., review conferences, various discussion and decision-making forums related to the START and Intermediate-Range Nuclear Forces (INF) agreements, the Treaty on Conventional Armed Forces in Europe (CFE) and Open Skies Treaties, and the Vienna Document on Confidence- and Security-Building Measures).

2. Negotiations that aimed to address some pending arrangements continued regardless of the fundamental change in underlying strategic relations. START-2 and several European arms-control arrangements were pending or required further elaboration upon the end of the Cold War.

3. It was partly objectively necessary, and it was partly thought necessary that some commitments be expanded to countries that were not parties to them. This happened with the START-1 Treaty when the Soviet Union collapsed and left several nuclear successor states behind, just as it did with the CFE, which was confined to members of partly moribund alliances. The former was turned into a multilateral agreement involving the US and the four nuclear successor states of the Soviet Union; the goal of the latter seemed to be the "harmonization" of arms-control commitments in the Commission on Security and Cooperation in Europe (CSCE) context.

4. Since the early 1990s, conflicting parties have considered the adoption of arms-control measures as part of broad settlements to conclude major conflicts. Such regulations were adopted on the basis of the 1995 Dayton agreement, extending to both confidence-building and arms limitations. Although there are not enough cases to substantiate whether this is the right venue for the future of arms control, it is certainly considered in the context of those conflicts that might be found "ripe for resolution."[3]

5. Measures have been considered that would have a direct bearing upon the security perception of people rather than that of governments. The ban on anti-personnel landmines has been universally adopted. Further consideration is now being given to mines other than anti-personnel landmines (MOTAPM), whereas the regulation of small arms and light weapons is being considered in a variety of regional contexts. The limitation of Man-Portable Air Defense Systems (MANPADS) is also being considered, and some soft documents have already been agreed upon in the framework of the Organization for Security and Co-operation in Europe (OSCE).

6. Another new avenue has been witnessed in terms of export control and other transfer control measures. This led to the British initiative to agree on a Treaty on Arms Trade. It remains to be seen whether the apparent US opposition does not prevent the arms trade treaty from blossoming.

7. Among the ideas that have flourished in the post-Cold War era, projects have appeared that have contributed to the reduction of the capacities of some actors with the help of others, like the US-Soviet (later US-post-Soviet) and the multilateral-post-Soviet Cooperative Threat Reduction (CTR) frameworks. Although they have flourished for some time, it is clear by now that their prospects would be far better if the state whose abundant capacities were limited/reduced/eliminated would cooperate by starting out with the view that its own capacity may also be of concern and that transparency does not jeopardize its national security. Such programs peaked when those conditions were present. Due to broader political changes, one can see that some elements of the CTR frameworks are being maintained, in relation to scrapping submarines, for example, while others have been reduced.

Each argument could contribute to some level of the continuation of arms control. It is clear, however, that except for those measures that are considered in the framework of human security, export controls, and CTR, others have rather served to keep the arms-control business going, preventing the once so mighty arms-control establishments from withering and, in the end, vanishing.

3. Dilemmas

For the past decade and a half, arms control has been facing the dilemma of retaining its relevance in international relations. The dilemma stems from the fact that the fundamental conflict underlying arms control has changed both in terms of its content and its geographic scope. Although it has interstate elements, its core is a conflict between states and non-state actors. This conflict cannot be influenced by means of arms control. There are interstate conflicts, however, where arms control could play a role. Those conflicts could be grouped as follows: (1) conflicts between the developed world, including the unipolar power and lesser powers. It is the intention of the former to enforce certain values; behavioral patterns, as declared; and certain interests, as often practiced; (2) conflicts between states in regions where arms control does not have strong roots, if any. In the former case, arms control is impossible; in the latter, it is seldom deemed necessary.

Arms control has been facing the dilemma of retaining its relevance. The first response measures contributed to the survival of arms control in the 1990s and resulted in the largest number of arms-control agreements in any decade during the second half of the 20th century. It seems that the agenda of arms control that we knew – a set of legally or politically binding norms based on negotiations (they were seldom unilateral or reciprocated unilaterally) – has been exhausted. The fact that the area that has flourished and gained the most importance since the end of the Cold War, non-proliferation, has gained autonomy and is more often than not thought to be only loosely associated with arms control.

The reactions of the arms-control establishment aimed to broaden the scope of arms control. The major areas of development can be seen in cooperative measures that affect armaments, reforms of the defense sector, and modernization "fostered" by some leading democracies and their allies in various parts of the world. It is doubtless that they all have some arms-control relevance, though none of them completely resemble "traditional" arms control.

The broadening of the scope of arms control has underlined its cohesion both in terms of the methods applied and the outcome. Arms control has become a concept with ill-defined contours. This has raised the question of whether what we call arms control is simply a linguistic tradition, whether our way of thinking is not too firmly rooted in the Cold War tradition. It is certainly difficult to get beyond philosophical and historical questions in arms control. Either arms control is a broad-ranging, if not all-embracing, concept that can be filled with adequate substance, or it is identified in the sense of the Cold War tradition and is largely hollow.

The dilemma is exacerbated by the fact that the new measures put forward and in some cases agreed upon have led to a situation where arms control has become a less autonomous component of international security. It borders upon other issues of international politics and on other professional communities. Namely, its post-Cold

War successes are linked to humanitarian arms control and export control where it is closely linked with the humanitarian community[4] and with the business community. There, genuine military considerations are less prominent. Not even broader security considerations could rid themselves from other influences.

4. Implications

The major implication of the above is that arms control is in relative decline and adjustment. Furthermore, it has become a largely professional matter that seldom finds its place on top of the political agenda. Since Europe, the region with the richest arms-control *acquis*, is not developing it further, it faces difficulties in propagating methods to apply elsewhere *mutatis mutandis*. This is a highly regrettable side effect of the general decline of traditional arms control.

One of the implications of the rearrangement of international power relations is that the conclusion of arms control agreements, which was a contributing factor of status in the international system, has vanished. Consequently, the status of the unipolar power would not be affected by concluding symbolic arms-control agreements. Others have occasionally been interested in such an arrangement.[5]

The lasting decline of arms control seems to be due to the coincidence of two sets of factors: the change in the security situation that resulted in the emergence of problems that could be affected only marginally by arms-control measures, if at all, and the decline of other problems where arms control played a relevant role. In the post-Cold War era, the world does not give prominence to arms control among the solutions to security problems. The decline of arms control has thus been primarily due to objective factors. It has been aggravated by the reaction of arms-control establishments in some cases. Generals are not the only ones who fight the last war and prepare plans accordingly. It is also arms controllers who want to avert the last conflict through agreed measures rather than by focusing on new challenges. If arms control could be shaped so that it could contribute to post-conflict settlement, or even better if it could play a role in the prevention of conflict, then it might regain some of its lost influence. The words of James Ferguson, written 15 years ago, that arms control "must necessarily remain meaningless in a high tension environment, whereas in a low tension environment, it becomes superfluous,"[6] have proved correct. Arms control is doomed in the narrow Cold War sense of the word, at least for some time to come.

5. Future Trajectories/Scenarios

There is reason to keep the objective, subjective, and incidental factors separate from one another. There is no reason to assume that the objective factors will change any time soon, i.e., the dominant players and conflict types will likely remain the same. One should not exclude the potential change of subjective factors. Although a new government in Washington may not bring about revolutionary changes and may not give arms control a pivotal role, it may well feel less animosity toward negotiated, legally binding security measures.

More importantly, experience shows that, not only can the world at large not gain influence in strategic matters in Washington without engagement, but the US also cannot gain influence in the world without engagement either. This recognition may lead the US government to engage in security matters with regimes it has declared "rogue" for some time. It is more of a question whether the animosity of the other party could be overcome soon. Arms control, as part of such talks, may be instrumental not necessarily with the intention of concluding an agreement but rather of conducting professional negotiations on security matters. (This is being half-heartedly pursued with North Korea, though not yet with Iran.) Nuclear arms control in the US-Russian context could regain some of its relevance and may be heading to further reductions of arsenals. Formal agreements might be advocated by Russia for symbolic reasons, although the current trend is going in the opposite direction.

In the regional context, there is some hope that some subregions will gradually develop a security *acquis* with arms control as part and parcel. This may hold for Central Asia that agreed upon a nuclear free weapon zone lately and for the Gulf region. In South Asia, negotiations on a broad range of confidence-building measures, including nuclear safety in the case of India and Pakistan, may well be necessary. The same would also be desirable in other high tension areas/environments. Regrettably, there the chances are worse than in South Asia. It is difficult to find a credible "honest broker" who could end the stalemate. It is a fact that the regionalization of security in the Asia-Pacific context could foster such soft arms-control processes. It is open to question, however, whether there is a chance to move from the subregional to the regional in the foreseeable future.

In the European context, the continent may continue to explore "exporting" its arms-control *acquis* while keeping a number of pending issues on its own arms-control agenda, like the pending status of the Adaptation Agreement to the CFE Treaty.

Overall, there is no reason to assume that the current role of arms control will change fundamentally any time soon.

6. Policy Recommendations

1. It is necessary to recognize the reduced role of arms control in the post-Cold War environment.

   The decline of arms control has been primarily due to objective reasons. The main underlying conflict sources of the post-Cold War era (intra-state insurgencies and strife, terrorism) cannot be affected by traditional means of arms control developed during the Cold War.

2. A close analysis should be carried out to determine which area of arms control has retained or (re-)gained residual political significance and hence where resources should be concentrated.

3. Consideration should be given to the question of which areas of traditional arms-control methods are still applicable for reasons of process (engagement of parties, transparency) and outcome (negotiated settlement).

4. Consideration should be given to the question of how traditional methods of arms control relate to non-traditional ones, including military coercion. Consideration should be given to an adequate mix of means and methods in arms control in the broad sense.

5. Arms control should be more closely integrated into human-security and non-proliferation efforts in the broadest sense, ranging from export controls of conventional dual-use technologies to nuclear non-proliferation.

6. The US should give up its reservations concerning arms control. It is necessary to thoroughly review the overall consequences of the Bush administration's animosity toward arms control and legally binding international measures more broadly. The next administration should act on the basis of conclusions drawn and return to the arms-control scene selectively and proactively.

7. The agenda of arms control should be broadened partly through the reintegration of non-proliferation in arms control without losing the *differentia specifica* of non-proliferation. Arms control should get closer to the broad category of arms regulation as enshrined in the United Nations Charter.

References

[1] Most non-conservative commentators on US security policy mention this concerning the administration of George W. Bush. According to John Steinbruner, "U.S. security policy is currently dominated by a political faction that rejects any meaningful dependence on legal regulation and asserts the right to initiate military action on behalf of national interest regardless of international legal justification." See J.D. Steinbruner, "Can Arms Control Be Revived?," *Arms Control Today,* March 2005, http://www.armscontrol.org/act/2005_BookReview.asp?print; Stephen E. Miller quotes John Bolton, who made the point that "America rejects the illusionary protections of unenforceable treaties." See S.E. Miller, "Skepticism Triumphant: The Bush Administration and the Waning of Arms Control," in H.J. Giessmann, R. Kuzniar, Z. Lachowski (eds.), *International Security in a Time of Change: Threats – Concepts – Institutions* (Baden-Baden: Nomos Verlag, 2004), p. 21. Stanley Hoffman takes the view that, "As for international law, it is seen as little more than words on paper, unless it is backed by force." S. Hoffman, "America Goes Backward," *The New York Review of Books,* June 12, 2003, p. 75.

[2] Memorably, the so-called Geneva Call aims to bring some insurgent groups under the edifice of the ban on anti-personnel landmines. Their record has demonstrated how tedious it is to attempt to address non-state actors in arms control.

[3] Neil MacFarlane contemplates this in the context of Nagorno-Karabakh, if Armenia and Azerbaijan ever find a solution to their long-standing conflict. N. MacFarlane, "Arms Control, Conflict and Peace Settlements: The Caucasus," in K. Krause and F. Tanner (eds.), *Arms Control and Contemporary Conflicts: Challenges and Responses* (Geneva: HEI, 2001), p. 50.

[4] This could be perceived clearly when the convention on anti-personnel landmines was negotiated. Humanitarian consideration prevailed over security concerns in a number of instances.

[5] This is how the so-called START-3 agreement was agreed upon by Russia and the US and signed by Presidents Vladimir Putin and George W. Bush.

[6] J. Ferguson, "The Changing Arms Control Agenda: New Meanings, New Players," *Arms Control,* September 1991, p. 197.

CHAPTER 13

EDITORIAL OF POLICY BRIEF ON ARMS CONTROL IN A
GLOBALIZED WORLD

NAYEF R.F. AL-RODHAN

Dr. Nayef R.F. Al-Rodhan is Senior Scholar in Geostrategy and Director of the Program on the Geopolitical Implications of Globalization and Transnational Security at the Geneva Centre for Security Policy, Geneva, Switzerland

1. Review and Critique

Since the end of the Cold War, arms control has slipped from center stage. This is, at least in part, due to the priorities of leading nuclear powers. Rather than being marginalized, nuclear weapons continue to be perceived by some as essential to managing today's security challenges. "Nuclear orthodoxy"[1] has developed through major nuclear powers seeking to retain their global status as a nuclear state on a number of levels. In other words, the development of modern nuclear arsenals, such as China, is countered by the former superpowers desire to maintain nuclear weaponry.

As Brad Roberts notes, there are also states that are determined to gain strategic leverage through the possession of weapons of mass destruction.[2] Since the Nuclear Non-Proliferation Treaty (NPT) was established in 1968, a number of countries have joined (or will possibly soon join) the ranks of nuclear states (India, Israel, Iran, North Korea, and Pakistan). The possibility of the proliferation of nuclear weapons destabilizing various regions is of paramount concern.[3] Yet, arms control has traditionally been centered on Europe. In regions outside of the Euro-Atlantic area, regional arms-control initiatives have been largely confined to participation in global arms-control measures. While some indigenous arms-control measures have emerged, such as confidence-building in border zones in Central Asia, they remain elementary and of marginal importance.[4]

In addition, the risk of non-state actors gaining control of weapons of mass destruction has become an increasing worry.[5] The diffusion of materials, technologies, and expertise that have both civilian and military use complicates the task of preventing the spread of nuclear technologies or materials to non-state actors.[6] As Mohamed ElBaradei has pointed out, this is particularly worrisome since the present system of export controls relies on informal arrangements that are non-binding, limited in membership, and, moreover, fail to include many countries with expanding industrial capacities.[7] New supplier nations also render the task of preventing non-state proliferators all the more complex, given that they are not bound by the non-proliferation obligations to which parties to the NPT adhere to.

This does not mean, however, that arms control has ceased to be relevant. The demise of the superpower arms race has simply resulted in its being deployed in less prominent areas than before. Arms control today tends to be associated with the concept of human security and security-sector reform.[8] As Pál Dunay points out in his policy brief, one of the major dilemmas facing arms control is whether to redefine itself in broader terms by integrating arms-control-relevant activities or to continue to be defined in narrow terms and accept a certain loss of relevance, at least in relative terms.[9]

2. Dilemmas and Our Recommendations

The emergence of new nuclear nations implies that arms control must expand its geographical scope. It must also adjust to changes in the fundamental conflicts underlying arms control. In what follows, we highlight eight dilemmas related to this issue and eight corresponding recommendations that may contribute to appropriate policy choices.

A major challenge facing arms control is the difficulty posed by the de facto nuclear-weapons states. As non-members of the NPT, monitoring technological developments within these states and preventing them from proliferating further is, as mentioned, particularly difficult. Responding appropriately to these new nuclear-weapons powers will be vital to encouraging regional arms-control measures. Yet, members of the NPT face the problem of effectively dealing with the three nuclear states that remain outside the Treaty without appearing to reward them with cooperation. First, outstanding conflicts should be resolved in order to lessen the perceived need for

nuclear deterrence. Regional conflict prevention, including confidence-building measures, should also be encouraged. As Pál Dunay suggests, these states ought to be pressed to commit to the non-proliferation obligations that the parties to the NPT adhere to. Since the ability of states to do so is likely to vary, assistance should be given to those with limited governance capacities to help them to ensure the safety of fissile material and reactors in a verifiable manner.

As alluded to earlier, one of the major problems facing the arms-control regime is the increased relevance attached to non-state actors. Preventing proliferation of dual-use technology to these actors, which escape the state-based NPT, is an especially thorny issue. We suggest that multilateral security cooperation should be encouraged. One option would be to reform the control system in order to better monitor trade flows, as well as to improve intelligence sharing among states and non-state actors. Preventing proliferation to non-state actors will also require long-term measures aimed at preventing states from selling to them.

A sizeable dilemma faced by policy makers is whether to continue to use traditional arms-control tools or whether to broaden the scope of arms control. Preventing non-state actors from acquiring nuclear weapons ultimately means reducing the gap between rich and poor within and between states. This implies expanding arms control to encompass a broader range of activities that will overlap, at the very least, development concerns. It is, therefore, imperative to promote greater cooperation between relevant sectors. The establishment of a United Nations (UN) office for arms control would also encourage the implementation of comprehensive, coordinated, multilateral arms-control efforts.

Faced with new actors, including the new nuclear states and non-state actors, some states may be tempted to engage in unilateral, punitive action based on narrowly defined self-interest. Yet, this threatens to undermine the effectiveness and credibility of multilateral arms-control endeavors. In order to prevent this from occurring, states should develop agreed criteria for multilateral arms control based on equality between states. They should also avoid the hypocrisy of selling to some states and preventing proliferation to others.

3. Conclusion

Perhaps the biggest difficulty facing arms control is the lack of consensus on how best to respond to threats to security and stability. No agreement yet exists as to how to respond to determined state proliferators, as well as non-state proliferators. This has resulted in new-found rationales for nuclear weapons among some of the original nuclear powers. If arms control is to retain its relevance, it must expand its geographical scope. It must also embrace non-traditional activities that overlap with development and security-sector reform.

References

[1] J. Krause, "The Crisis in Nuclear Arms Control," in J. Krause and A. Wenger (eds.), *Nuclear Weapons into the 21st Century: Current Trends and Future Prospects* (Bern, etc.: Peter Lang, 2001), p. 26.

[2] B. Roberts, "Rethinking N + 1," *National Interest*, Spring 1998.

[3] Krause and Wenger, *op. cit.*, note 1, pp. 17-19.

[4] For the brief in its entirety, please see Chapter 12.

[5] See, for instance, A.B. Carter, J. Deutch, and P. Zelikow, "Catastrophic Terrorism: Tackling the New Danger," *Foreign Affairs*, November/December 1998; Roberts, *op. cit.*, note 2.

[6] *Ibid.*

[7] M. ElBaradei, "Nuclear Non-Proliferation: Global Security In A Rapidly Changing World," Statements of the Director General (IAEA), Washington, DC, June 21, 2004, available at http://www.iaea.org/NewsCenter/Statements/2004/ebsp2004n004.html.

[8] See N. MacFarlane, "Arms Control, Conflict and Peace Settlements: The Caucasus," in K. Krause and F. Tanner (eds.), *Arms Control and Contemporary Conflicts: Challenges and Responses* (Geneva: HEI, 2001).

CHAPTER 14

ENERGY SECURITY, GLOBALIZATION, AND GLOBAL SECURITY

JOHN C. GAULT

Dr. John C. Gault is President of John Gault SA and Associate Faculty Member at the Geneva Centre for Security Policy, Geneva, Switzerland

Abstract
This article is a brief overview of critical issues in energy security that could affect globalization and global security. Energy trade continues to expand and energy delivery networks are becoming increasingly complex. Energy exporters, transit countries, and importers can all suffer from system interruptions. As our mutual dependence on extensive energy networks grows, so does our vulnerability to energy shortages. Policies such as diversification of trade routes and of sources of supply, as well as maintenance of strategic reserves, are necessary, but not sufficient, protections against energy interruptions. The article concludes with a series of policy recommendations for governments (whether of energy-exporting, -importing, or transit countries) to improve the security of energy supply; to encourage adequate investment in energy infrastructure; and to minimize the likelihood of, and damage caused by, energy system breakdowns.

1. Policy Challenges

The energy industry has been global in scale since long before the current wave of globalization. In December 1861, only two years after the first oil well was drilled in Titusville, Pennsylvania, the brig *Elizabeth Watts* sailed from Philadelphia to London carrying barrels of kerosene. For much of the remainder of the 19th century, more than one-third of United States (US) oil production was exported.[1]

International oil trade was accompanied by international oil investment. In the 1870s, the Swedish Nobel brothers invested in oil production and transportation in Azerbaijan, and in the 1880s, the Paris branch of the Rothschild family financed the construction of a railway to carry oil from Baku to Batum on the Black Sea, from where it could be shipped to Western Europe.[2]

Although the energy industry thus has long experience in cross-border trade and investment, the current wave of globalization has revealed new stresses and new policy challenges that arise for the following reasons:

- The share of energy traded internationally is increasing. For example, less than half of global oil production in 1965 was traded inter-regionally; in 2004, the share was about 60 percent, and this share will continue to grow.[3] Similar upward trends can be observed in the trade of coal, natural gas, and electricity.

- The average distance transported is also increasing. Domestic oil and gas production in major consuming regions such as the United States, Europe, and China is declining and is being replaced by imports from ever-greater distances. This trend, too, will continue.

- The volume of investment required to meet growing energy demand is rising. The International Energy Agency (IEA) has projected that $16 trillion (in dollars of the year 2000) will be needed to meet global growth in energy requirements through the year 2030.[4]

- Idle capacity at all levels has been shrinking. Global trends of market liberalization have encouraged competition, forcing energy firms to achieve ever-higher rates of infrastructure utilization. At the same time, environmental concerns have delayed or prevented some new investments in, for example, oil refining and electric power generation.

- Evidence continues to accumulate to support the hypothesis that combustion of fossil fuels contributes to global warming.

- Both energy consumers and producers appear increasingly concerned about the risks of interruptions in the energy supply chain. These fears have been enhanced not only by bottlenecks in oil-refining capacity and limited idle crude oil production capacity, but also by electricity blackouts in the northeastern United States, Italy, and elsewhere; the brief interruption in Russia's supply of natural gas to Ukraine; the decline in Iraqi oil production since the 2003 invasion; and other geopolitical events.

The perceptions of producers and consumers that security risks are increasing are understandable. The growth in volumes of energy moving ever-greater distances, across additional political borders, and through narrow choke-points (such as the Straits of Hormuz and Malacca) renders energy supplies more vulnerable to sudden interruption. Over the long run, restrictions on investment in energy infrastructure, whether for environmental, political, or other reasons, remain a serious concern.

One further challenge, beyond the scope of this brief overview of energy security and globalization, must be mentioned. According to the IEA, about 2.4 billion people in developing countries rely on biomass for their basic energy supplies, and some 1.6 billion people, mostly in sub-Saharan Africa and South Asia, have no access to electricity.[5] Energy inequalities are only one aspect of income inequalities; the two are closely interrelated. Without access to modern fuels, people cannot achieve levels of productivity sufficient to lift themselves out of poverty. In the long run, overcoming this energy gap may be even more critical to global security than resolving all the other energy security challenges discussed in this essay.

2. Responses

As the stresses on global energy trade have grown and become more apparent, governments and international organizations have responded. Governments of major oil-importing countries responded to the Arab oil embargo of 1973 by creating the International Energy Agency with its emergency plan for sharing oil supply shortages through coordinated demand reduction and the release of strategic stocks. This emergency plan was implemented, for example, in early 1991, during the Iraqi occupation of Kuwait, and in 2005, following the hurricane-caused interruptions in Gulf of Mexico oil supplies.

The strategic stocks of the Organisation for Economic Co-operation and Development (OECD) countries today amount to over

1.4 billion barrels.[6] IEA members that are net importers of oil are required to maintain the equivalent of 90 days of the preceding year's imports. The European Union requires member states to hold the equivalent of 90 days' consumption of three specific petroleum products.[7] The governments of India and China, both increasingly dependent on oil imports, are planning strategic petroleum stockpiles, although neither country has begun filling such reserves (as of March 2006).[8]

Governments of oil-importing countries have sought to diversify sources of energy supplies and transport routes in the hope of improving energy security. Perhaps the most widely publicized of these efforts was the United States' official encouragement of the construction of the Baku-Tbilisi-Ceyhan (BTC) crude oil pipeline from Azerbaijan to the Turkish Mediterranean coast as an alternative to shipping Azeri crude oil either through Russia or through Iran. For many years, the Japanese government has looked forward to the development of Russian oil and natural gas at Sakhalin Island as a way of reducing the country's heavy dependence on Middle East supplies. For the same reason, the Japanese government has tried to persuade Russia that a future oil pipeline from Siberian fields should terminate directly at the Russian port of Nakhodka, thus facilitating oil export to Japan.[9]

Governments of energy-exporting countries have similarly sought to diversify markets and transport routes for security reasons. Iraq opened its Strategic North-South Pipeline in 1975 and its pipeline via Turkey to Ceyhan in 1977 in response to Syrian interruptions of the existing pipeline from Iraq to the Mediterranean at Banias.[10] Similarly, Iraqi crude was to be exported by a dedicated pipeline (IPSA-2) via Saudi Arabia to Yanbu on the Red Sea, but this pipeline was inaugurated only months before Iraq's invasion of Kuwait in 1990 forced its closure.[11]

One may reasonably interpret Saudi Arabia's construction of both crude oil and natural gas liquids pipelines from the Eastern Province to Yanbu, and Algeria's construction of additional trans-Mediterranean gas pipelines as strategic diversifications to ensure that some export revenue would continue even if other routes were to be interrupted.

A current example is Russia's proposal to export natural gas to Germany and possibly other European countries via a Northern

European (Baltic) Gas Pipeline, which would follow a sub-sea route to avoid passing through either Ukraine or Belarus.

While climate change may not appear to be an energy-related security issue, it has the potential to become one. As evidence accumulates to suggest that the combustion of fossil fuels contributes to global warming, countries suffering damages may blame other countries emitting high levels of greenhouse gases. The Framework Convention on Climate Change and the Kyoto Protocol were intended to achieve an equitable sharing of the burden of reducing greenhouse-gas emissions, but the Kyoto Protocol was not all-inclusive, and many signatories probably will fail to meet their Protocol targets. Moreover, major exporters of fossil fuels argue that their national interests will be damaged by measures taken to discriminate against such fuels.

3. Dilemmas

The maintenance of strategic reserves and the diversification of energy sources and supply routes are important policies that no doubt will continue to be pursued. However, both have their limitations.

For example, strategic stocks of natural gas are more expensive to maintain than stocks of oil, and not all countries have natural underground storage opportunities. Above-ground storage in the form of liquefied natural gas (LNG) is even more expensive. Hence, a rule requiring each importing country to maintain a given number of days of gas (imports or consumption) in storage would have a highly unequal impact.

As another example, withdrawals from strategic reserves (whether of oil or of gas) are limited by the capacity of the installed infrastructure. This infrastructure appears to be ample in the case of IEA members' strategic oil reserves, which can be drawn down at up to 12 million barrels per day for the first month, and at declining rates thereafter.[12] To the extent that governments decide to maintain strategic stocks of natural gas, adequate drawdown and delivery infrastructure must be installed to meet emergency calls on stored gas.

An analogous limitation arises with diversified supply sources and routes. In the case of petroleum or LNG, it may be relatively easy to re-direct a tanker already *en route* to deliver its cargo to energy-deprived regions. In the case of natural gas pipelines or electricity transmission lines, however, an interruption of one source or facility at a time of high consumption cannot be accommodated if no alternative facility has idle capacity. The alternative sources of supply will, under such circumstances, already be operating at or near their capacity limits.

The dilemma is that private investors in liberalized markets have little incentive to invest in non-revenue-producing idle capacity. Competition forces companies to cut costs and to achieve high utilization rates of their facilities. Governments must therefore employ either carrots or sticks to ensure that idle capacity is maintained at all levels of energy supply chains.

Oil-importing countries long benefited from a cushion of idle crude oil production capacity in major exporting countries. This idle capacity came into existence during the 1980s due to events in oil-importing countries: economic recession, expansion of domestic oil production (especially in Alaska and the North Sea), energy-conservation and fuel-substitution measures (such as expansion of coal-fired and nuclear power generation). Gradually, as oil demand expanded, this idle capacity in major exporting countries shrank. Recent oil price increases have been blamed, in part, on buyer nervousness resulting from a smaller cushion of idle production capacity worldwide.

Major oil-exporting countries have announced plans to increase production capacities at a pace faster than expected growth of global demand, so the cushion of idle capacity should increase in coming years. However, such expansion plans may be delayed if oil exporters fear that their investment will never be used. Oil exporters remain concerned about the "security of demand," in the face of statements by governments of oil-importing countries that they will seek to reduce dependence on imported oil. Major oil-consuming countries appear, so far, unwilling to recognize the value of, or contribute to the burden of, maintaining idle production capacity upstream.

Adding to the above dilemmas is the accumulating evidence that the use of force to protect complex energy delivery networks from sabotage cannot guarantee total security. For example, Shining Path guerrillas in Peru repeatedly blew up electric pylons; guerrillas in Colombia frequently interrupted flow in the Cano Limon oil pipeline; rebels in the Niger Delta have forced the closure of major oil transportation facilities; and the armies occupying Iraq have been unable to prevent nearly continuous sabotage of electric power and petroleum infrastructures. Good intelligence can help to prevent some such attacks, but a determined and perseverant saboteur will eventually succeed. The strategic response to this dilemma cannot be exclusively military; it must include political solutions to political problems.

4. Implications

Energy trade has expanded during the current wave of globalization, and threats to energy security have increased as well. For several decades, the threats were partially disguised by the existence of ample idle crude oil production capacity in major oil-exporting countries. Consumer-country responses to energy security threats consisted primarily of maintaining strategic petroleum stocks and diversifying supply sources and routes. Governments of consuming countries believed, at least tacitly, that in the event of a serious disruption of oil supplies, military intervention would be the ultimate, and a sufficient, resort.

The adequacy of these responses is now in doubt. As the length and complexity of energy supply lines have grown – not only for oil but also for natural gas, coal, and electricity – the vulnerability of energy sources, transmission systems, transformation sites, trading hubs and storage facilities has grown as well. New approaches to energy security are required.

Among the most urgent requirements for all governments are:

- More accurate, timely, and transparent data on energy supply, demand, production, and transformation volumes, as well as reserves;

- Studies to identify critical nodes in energy production, transmission, and distribution networks in order to provide idle capacity in the most efficient manner;

- Continuous updating of data on electric power generation facilities' and other major fuel users' fuel-switching capabilities, on-site stocks of alternative fuels, and the potential emissions consequences of fuel-switching;

- Rationing plans to minimize the human and economic cost of an energy supply interruption; and

- Greater international cooperation in planning for, avoiding, and minimizing the consequences of fuel supply interruptions.

5. Future Trajectories/Scenarios

The most widely relied-upon forecasts indicate that global consumption of hydrocarbons will continue to expand at least for the next two decades.[13] The pace of this growth will depend upon many factors, including oil prices and the policies of consumer governments.

While some analysts argue that production of conventional crude oil either has peaked or soon will,[14] if current investment plans are implemented, oil production capacity will expand faster than demand, at least to the end of the present decade.[15] Additional capacity from tar sands and heavy-oil deposits will complement technological improvements and improved recovery rates from conventional oil reservoirs over a much longer time horizon.

Governments of major consuming countries will likely seek to increase their production of energy from domestic sources, using such incentives as: higher taxes on hydrocarbons, tax deductions and/or subsidies for non-hydrocarbon fuels, regulations, and other methods. Governments will justify these programs on both security and environmental grounds. Nuclear power generation will continue to expand in France, Japan, The Republic of Korea, China, and it is possible that new nuclear power plants will be constructed in countries where there has been no expansion for many years, such as the United States.

National (i.e., state-owned) oil companies (NOCs) will become more prominent in the oil and gas industry. Current high oil prices have given producing-country NOCs greater financial strength. Some NOCs now feel they have less need to attract partners for exploration and production activities from among international oil companies. At the same time, consuming-country NOCs from China and India have acquired oil and gas exploration and production rights in a wide variety of host countries.

The increasingly prominent role of NOCs has alarmed journalists and politicians in some major oil-importing countries.

Opposition in the United States Congress, for example, recently forced the China National Offshore Oil Company (CNOOC) to abandon its offer to acquire the California-based Unocal Corporation.[16] Given the large amounts of investment funds required for oil and gas facilities in the coming years, however, the willingness of Chinese and Indian companies to make such investments should be welcome. All consumers will benefit from increases in global production capacity.

6. Policy Recommendations

Given the long history of cross-border trade and investment in the energy industry, it is unlikely that energy security concerns will reverse the industry's expanding global activities, in spite of the many policy challenges and dilemmas listed above.

Nevertheless, steps can be taken by governments – individually and collectively – to improve energy security for their own citizens and for the world as a whole. This is not a zero-sum effort; if appropriate policies are instituted, the improvement of one country's energy security need not be at the expense of other countries'.

Among the most urgent policies are:

1. *Coordinating the development and maintenance of idle capacity all along energy supply chains.* This means undertaking studies of entire networks as a whole, from the producing facilities to the end-consumers, to determine the points of greatest vulnerability requiring the greatest protection, and the points where idle capacity could most efficiently be maintained. Such an undertaking requires high-level cooperation among energy-producing, transit, and -consuming countries. Given the intricacy of energy supply systems, energy security must be sought on a network-wide basis, rather than within narrow national boundaries.

2. *Oil-importing countries that do not yet maintain strategic stocks of petroleum should begin building such stocks.* All countries, whether or not members of the IEA, benefit from the IEA's oil-storage and emergency-response

system, and all countries should therefore share the burden.

3. *Improving the quality of data reporting, analysis, and forecasting of consumption, stocks, production, production capacities, transportation and transformation capacities, and reserves.* The Joint Oil Data Initiative (JODI), inaugurated by King Abdullah of Saudi Arabia on November 19, 2005,[17] needs the support of all governments, and should be expanded to include production capacities, reserves, and other data not currently included in the program. A similar program for natural gas data should be launched.

4. *Governments of both energy-producing and -consuming countries must agree to prohibit the use of energy trade interruptions (or threats thereof) to achieve political ends.* Sanctions imposed on energy exporters and embargos imposed on energy importers are equally disruptive and contribute to an atmosphere of fear about energy security. Such fear can lead to unwarranted price volatility and to uneconomic and unnecessary investment in expensive alternatives.

5. *Governments of both energy-producing and -consuming countries, as well as governments of transit countries, should encourage companies to participate in interlocking ownerships of upstream, transit, and downstream facilities.* Arrangements whereby companies (whether private or public) from energy-importing countries become shareholders in upstream facilities in energy-exporting countries, and vice versa, have long been common in the natural gas industry, especially with regard to trade in liquefied natural gas. By ensuring that all parties have everything to gain from supply continuity, and everything to lose from a supply interruption, interlocking ownership contributes to energy supply security.

6. *All governments must provide regulations for identifying who is responsible in the event of a supply interruption.* For those governments pursuing domestic market liberalization policies, including "unbundling" of services in the gas and electricity sectors, it is critical to inform companies of their respective responsibilities for maintaining supply continuity, and of their liabilities in the event of interruptions. Only with such clear assignments of responsibility will companies be motivated to invest funds to minimize risks.

7. *Governments should strive for a comprehensive agreement on limiting greenhouse-gas emissions.* The Kyoto Protocol is not comprehensive because major countries are not participants. Whatever agreement succeeds the Kyoto Protocol must be comprehensive so investors everywhere will face a level playing field. A clear picture of the future investment environment will be needed if the required $16 trillion is to be drawn into the energy sector over the coming 25 years.

Acknowledgements

The author is grateful for the comments of Nordine Ait-Laoussine on a draft of this article.

References

[1] C. Tugendhat and A. Hamilton, *Oil, the Biggest Business* (London: Eyre Methuen, 1975) revised edition, p. 11.
[2] *Ibid.*, p. 35.
[3] "BP Statistical Review of World Energy," June 2006 is available online at www.bp.com/statisticalreview. Please see http://www.bp.com/liveassets/bp_internet/globalbp/globalbp_uk_english/publications/energy_reviews_2006/STAGING/local_assets/downloads/pdf/statistical_review_of_world_energy_full_report_2006.pdf.
[4] International Energy Agency, *World Energy Outlook 2004*, p. 72, please see http://www.iea.org/textbase/nppdf/free/2004/weo2004.pdf.
[5] *Ibid.*, p. 329.
[6] International Energy Agency, "Monthly Oil Market Report," March 2006, p. 59.
[7] International Energy Agency, "Fact Sheet: IEA Stocks and Emergency Response," available at http://www.iea.org.
[8] "Creation of strategic oil reserve sought," *The Hindu*, March 25, 2006; "China's planners slow timetable for oil reserves," *The Wall Street Journal*, March 7, 2006.
[9] "Putin hints at China oil pipeline," *BBC News*, March 23, 2006.

[10] P. Stevens, "Pipelines or pipe dreams? Lessons from the history of Arab transit pipelines," *The Middle East Journal*, Vol. 54, Issue 2, Spring 2000, pp. 224-241.
[11] *Ibid.*
[12] International Energy Agency, *op. cit.*, note 7.
[13] International Energy Agency, "World Energy Outlook" (various annual issues); United States Department of Energy, *International Energy Outlook* (various annual issues); A. Shihab-Eldin, M. Hamel, and G. Brennand, "Oil outlook to 2025," *OPEC Review*, Vol. 28, No. 3, September 2004, pp. 155-205.
[14] See, for example, K.S. Deffeyes, *Beyond Oil: The View from Hubbert's Peak* (New York: Hill and Wang, 2005).
[15] Cambridge Energy Research Associates, "Worldwide Liquids Capacity Outlook to 2010: Tight Supply or Excess of Riches?," May 2005.
[16] "CNOOC withdraws bid for Unocal, citing politics," *Oil and Gas Journal*, August 8, 2005, p. 29.
[17] See http://www.iea.org/Textbase/stats/jodi/NewsletterDec.pdf.

CHAPTER 15

EDITORIAL OF POLICY BRIEF ON ENERGY SECURITY, GLOBALIZATION, AND GLOBAL SECURITY

NAYEF R.F. AL-RODHAN

Dr. Nayef R.F. Al-Rodhan is Senior Scholar in Geostrategy and Director of the Program on the Geopolitical Implications of Globalization and Transnational Security at the Geneva Centre for Security Policy, Geneva, Switzerland

1. Review and Critique

The war in Iraq and the global dependence on oil and other sources of energy has led security of these resources towards an entirely new era. Now, more than ever, energy security rests on the cooperation of governments and multinational corporations to protect the transporttation of these goods as well as the employees who work in the field. As we have seen in the recent past with the kidnapped workers in Nigeria,[1] the security of pipelines and individuals has been compromised by groups wishing to disrupt the flow of oil out of these countries. In the modern world of trade and communication that has resulted in the continual globalization of markets and economic trends, energy reliability and pricing has also been affected. Consequently, the acquisition and maintenance of global energy supplies have taken their places once again on the lists of security priorities and geopolitical agendas.[2] There are a number of challenges facing oil-producing areas including: stability of oil exporting nations; terrorism; regional conflicts; the security of oil facilities; natural disasters; and ethnic conflicts and strife.[3] Each of these dilemmas affects the political and economic dimensions of globalization and has a far-reaching impact in our globalized world. Therefore, the connections between energy security and globalization become critical for any serious examination of global security and stability. Dr. Liam Fox recently noted the importance of this connection: "In the years ahead energy security, economic security and national security will be inextricably linked."[4] Therefore, these elements must be collectively understood and addressed.

As John Gault argues in his policy brief,[5] globalization, which has played a role in the energy industry since the 19th century,[6] has put new stresses on the international system; these new stresses have affected the global energy supply in important ways. Dr. Gault outlines a number of pertinent reasons, including increase in concern about the ability to ensure uninterrupted flows of oil via secure pipelines. He also points out that the distances over which these resources are transported are increasing and therefore the investment requirements for countries and companies is also rising, in order to meet the growing demand. All of these trends will continue, consequently forcing governments to respond in a number of ways. The creation of the International Energy Agency (IEA) was one such response in the 1970s; the current drive towards diversifying funds was also an important response mechanism mentioned by Dr. Gault.

Despite these responses, however, there are a limited number of options that are open to both oil importing and exporting countries, especially as the increase in attacks makes it more difficult and more expensive for energy suppliers to protect their networks. In describing how to combat these weaknesses, Dr. Fox emphasizes that "such a strategy will need to have three components: diversity in the type of fuels we use; diversity in the geographical sources of those fuels and the security structures that will guarantee the safe transport of these fuels."[7]

Dr. Gault argues that there are a number of urgent requirements for all governments, including timely and transparent data on energy supply, demand, and production. However, governments are mostly trying to deal with the global implications of potential disruption in energy supplies, especially as producing areas are threatened with closure as a result of potential environmental concerns.[8] In the emerging economies of India and China,[9] ensuring secure supply lines in order to meet global demands has reached a new level of importance. While each of these countries are still consuming less than, for example, the United States (US), the strain that this growing demand puts on the system in addition to current levels makes experts question the longevity of current global energy supplies.

The trends and trajectories related to global energy security are mostly fixated on the future including a world beyond oil as the single, dominant energy source. Countries and governments will need to work on diversifying their own energy sources as well as work on their own domestic production in order to secure vital flows of energy. The capacity of oil production will increase as the global market continues to invest in and demand the levels at which the world currently operates. The fluctuations in global demand which is increasing in countries such as India and China put pressure on the international system to resolve current and potential policy dilemmas. Dr. Gault's brief deals with these issues and makes strong recommendations on what governments need to do in order to minimize the security risks in the near-term future.

2. Dilemmas and Our Recommendations

Guaranteeing the flow of various forms of energy in and out of countries is a major security question for many states in the current debates about security. While it is true that globalization has created a new challenge for states, it has also created new opportunities for furthering global cooperation and for furthering state stability within the markets. For instance, improving the way in which governments coordinate their efforts in the energy industry will also assist in the cooperative measures which are developing or need to be further developed in other sectors. Concrete dilemmas and recommendations, therefore, present themselves in terms of the energy sector; we present those which we feel are the most important below.

While it is not necessary to describe in detail every dilemma and recommendation, it is important to note some general trends and trajectories. States are currently facing a financial investment dilemma to some degree when discussing the investment and development of renewable versus non-renewable energy sources.

Questions remain at the state level as to how to deal with the supply and demand aspect of energy security which quite often results in a disconnect between projections made by exporting states and importing states not having adequate or correct information. This also has implications for the resulting demand for increased production capacity and the potential need for states to make further investments into energy infrastructures. States must work towards better coordination and transparency of the relevant data which would lead to an energy "road map" for both producers and consumers. This

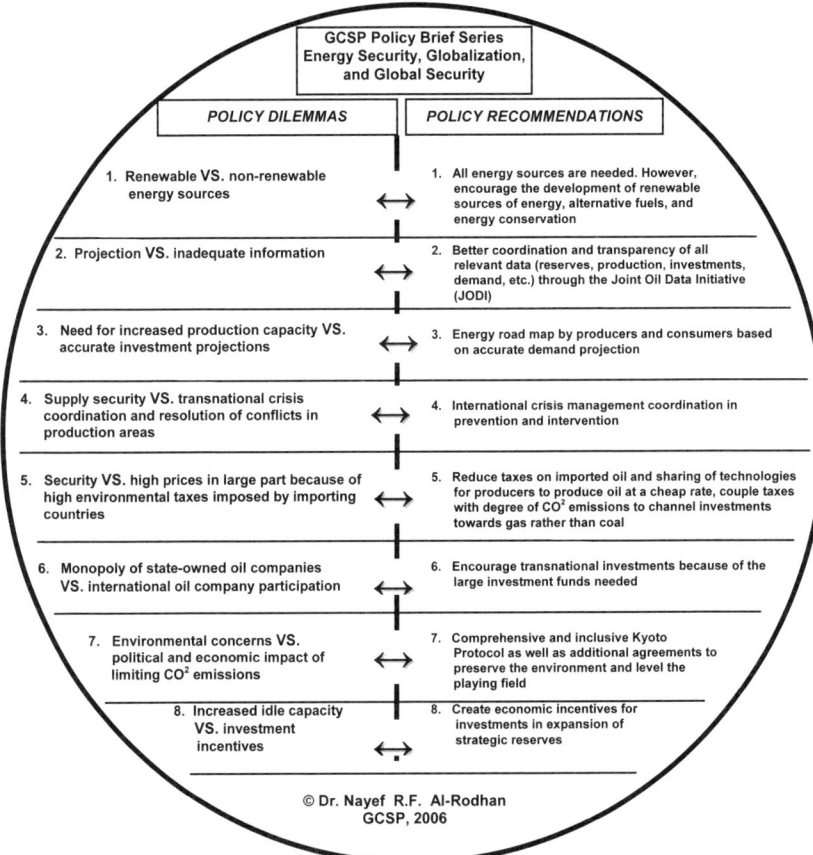

would reduce the vulnerability of both types of states and therefore build trust and faith in the negotiation process. When trust and faith in negotiations and communications are compromised, instability and fears of interrupted energy flows are created.

The environmental aspect of energy security is important and must not be left off any comprehensive list of dilemmas and subsequent recommendations. High taxes are often used as a tool in which to prevent increasing environmental damage. However, this will not sustain over the long term. Governments are in control of the taxing levels when it comes to dealing with import tariffs, contrary to the not uncommon popular belief that prices at the pump are mainly controlled by the Organization of the Petroleum Exporting Countries (OPEC). This misconception about the role of taxation in final consumer prices not only creates scapegoats but also promotes animosity and cultural suspicion towards OPEC countries and encourages insecurity in the general public. To promote the diversification of energy resources and move investments toward natural gas rather than continue the promotion of further coal investments and subsidies, taxes should be coupled with CO^2 emissions.

Politically and economically, states quite often face a dilemma when dealing with the question of limiting CO^2 emissions and multinational companies are sometimes reluctant to impose better emission standards themselves due to the costs involved. These types of sanctions must come from the top down and states must find a balance between economic, political, and environmental prosperity. A reduction in taxes on imported oil by importing governments, a sharing of technology for producers to produce oil at a cheaper rate, and ample taxes, where appropriate, will help to eliminate this problem. Additionally, a comprehensive and inclusive Kyoto Protocol, which should be adopted by all major importers and exporters of energy, would help to level the playing field.

Finally, the issue of state-owned oil companies must be addressed. Currently, the balance between state-owned oil companies and international oil company participation is creating a political dilemma for the global system. The agenda for both types of companies is naturally rooted in different goals and therefore largely affects those countries that depend heavily on oil and other exported energy supplies. There must be encouragement, both at the state and international level, for transnational investments, because of the large amount of funds required. A balance must be found between state and internationally run companies in order to minimize the national political and economic power as well as the influence in the international system as the demand for energy increases.

3. Conclusion

The concerns surrounding the security of energy flows both in its capacity to be produced effectively as well as the security guarantee for the transportation lines are vital issues for states in the near to long-term future. Political and economic incentives for investment as well as security measures must be at the top of the agenda for states. The international system is moving in the right direction in terms of energy security, but there are still areas which need to be looked at more thoroughly in order to ensure energy flows into the market for years to come.

References

[1] For more information on the kidnapping of oil workers in Nigeria in February of this year, please see "Oil Workers Kidnapped in Nigeria," *BBC News*, February 18, 2006, http://news.bbc.co.uk/2/hi/africa/4726680.stm.

[2] L. Beehner, "Global Oil Trends," *Council on Foreign Relations*, December 30, 2005, http://www.cfr.org/publication/9484/global_oil_trends.html.

[3] All of these dilemmas appear in A. Cordesman and K. Al-Rodhan, "The Changing Risks in Global Oil Supply and Demand: Crisis or Evolving Solutions?," *Center for Strategic and International Studies*, first working draft, October 3, 2005, at http://www.csis.org/media/csis/pubs/050930_globaloilrisks.pdf.

[4] Speech by Dr. Liam Fox, MP, Shadow Secretary of State for Defense, "Energy Security and Military Structures," given at Chatham House on May 22, 2006, please see http://www.chathamhouse.org.uk/pdf/research/niis/220506fox.pdf.

[5] For the brief in its entirety, please see Chapter 14.

[6] *Ibid*, John Gault argues in his opening paragraph, "In December 1861, only two years after the first oil well was drilled in Titusville, Pennsylvania, the brig *Elizabeth Watts* sailed from Philadelphia to London carrying barrels of kerosene." Please see the brief in its entirety for further information.

[7] Fox, *op. cit.*, note 4.

[8] BP has discussed shutting down its operations in Prudhoe Bay Alaska, North America's largest oil field, as a result of a scan that showed potentially serious corrosion on certain sections of the pipelines. Currently this is under discussion, but for a recent review of the topic, please see "BP Closer to Partial Reprieve," *CNN Money*, August 10, 2006, http://money.cnn.com/2006/08/10/news/economy/bp_prudhoe.reut/index.htm.

[9] For a full prediction by the IEA of where energy trends are heading, please see the most recent *World Energy Outlook*, available at http://www.worldenergyoutlook.org/.

CHAPTER 16

WATER, GLOBALIZATION, AND GLOBAL SECURITY

PETER H. GLEICK

Dr. Peter H. Gleick is President of the Pacific Institute, Oakland, California, United States

Abstract
Water has become a serious and challenging global issue, with local and regional political, economic, and social aspects. This paper reviews policy challenges, the consequences of unresolved water problems, and possible "soft path" solutions. Among the most pressing issues around water globalization is the controversial trend toward privatization, the failure to meet basic human needs for water, worsening ecological degradation, and the risk of international and subnational violence over shared water resources. Solutions to water problems exist, but scientists, policy makers, and the public must identify and overcome obstacles to implementing these solutions.

1. Policy Challenges

As we approach the end of the first decade of the 21st century, water-resource problems continue to present difficult human, environmental, political, and social challenges. In response to these challenges, a wide range of solutions, technologies, and policies have been proposed, but inadequate effort has been made to implement them. New thinking, new tools, and vigorous action are required in the coming years.

Perhaps the greatest unresolved water problem is the failure to meet basic human needs for water. More than a billion people still lack access to safe drinking water; more than 2.6 billion lack access to adequate sanitation.[1] The resulting toll in illness and death remains a major focus for international water institutions and governments. For example, water is one of the priorities for the Millennium Development Goals of the United Nations,[2] but it appears unlikely that these goals will be met.

Equally challenging is the growing risk of both international and subnational conflicts over water resources. Water resources are widely shared internationally, with more than 260 major international river basins, and few truly effective international agreements among conflicting parties.[3] As populations grow, conflicts over water allocation among different economic sectors and between political groups will also grow. As noted in the Water Conflict Chronology,[4] violence over water resources appears to be increasing, particularly among subnational groups.

The environmental consequences of poorly thought-out water management and use are also a major challenge. Aquatic ecosystems are under stress in many parts of the world due to excessive water withdrawals or water contamination resulting from inadequate water-quality regulation and monitoring. Unless the protection of aquatic ecosystems becomes a more fundamental part of water management, adverse impacts on a wide range of species are likely to grow.

Part of the challenge in meeting these goals is the lack of agreement on what to do. There are conflicting interests among the national and international actors, different models for water development, inadequate understanding of the risks and benefits of globalization, and uneven institutional capabilities in different regions of the world. Unless adequate approaches are developed and implemented, social, political, and economic unrest over fresh water will grow.

2. Responses

A wide range of responses to water problems have been proposed or tried, ranging from local to international efforts, privatization to improvement of governmental capabilities, and accelerated technological development to better-integrated management. No single approach has been agreed upon by governments or water managers, however, leading to inconsistent and uneven responses.

A major part of the attempt to satisfy human needs for water is the effort associated with the Millennium Development Goals, adopted by the United Nations in an effort to reduce poverty. Two of the goals are to reduce by half the proportion of people without access to safe and affordable water and sanitation by 2015.[5] The tools used to tackle these objectives vary widely but focus mostly on increased funding, more effective institutions, and educational efforts.

In the 1990s, some governments and international funding agencies, such as the World Bank, began looking to the private sector to help manage, fund, and operate water systems, particularly in regions where governments have failed to meet their responsibilities. A wide range of models for water privatization have been tried, in a wide variety of places, ranging from complete privatization of ownership and operation to far more limited models of simple private management of limited water services.[6] As noted below, the idea of privatizing water systems is very contentious for political, economic, and cultural reasons, but it remains a response that requires attention and evaluation. At the same time, it is increasingly apparent that the public opposition to privatization is strong when inadequate protection is given to the public interest.

Another traditional response to water problems has been investment in large-scale infrastructure in the form of large dams, aqueducts, and centralized water-treatment facilities. Such investments in the past have brought great benefits to hundreds of millions of people in the form of improved reliability and quality of water, improved resistance to droughts and floods, and a reduction in water-related diseases. Such large facilities, however, are increasingly controversial and expensive, and their often-ignored social and environmental consequences are beginning to force governments and communities to seek solutions that rely less on hard infrastructure and more on integrated water management and the "soft path" (see Policy Recommendations below).

In a related global trend, the failure to meet basic needs for safe water has spurred explosive growth in the use of bottled water, which now is a global phenomenon with sales approaching $100 billion annually.[7] Table 1 shows global bottled-water sales from 1996 to 2004. Controversy over the costs and environmental impact of bottled water is growing, but as long as governments fail to provide inexpensive, safe drinking water, the market for private water sales is likely to continue to grow.

For many water problems, one response is an increase in regional water-management efforts. For international watersheds, conflicts over water can be addressed by regional agreements, such as those under negotiation by the recent Nile Basin Initiative and the Mekong River Commission. These have met with mixed success. Some regions are trying to develop systems for managing river basins to get away from the mismatch between hydrologic boundaries and political borders.

Table 1: Global Bottled-Water Use, 1996-2004

Year	% Change	Thousands of Cubic Meters
1996	--	72,676
1997	11.00	80,649
1998	8.90	87,839
1999	12.10	98,459
2000	9.90	108,171
2001	9.90	118,864
2002	11.50	132,499
2003	9.40	144,925
2004(p.)	6.50	154,381

p. Preliminary
Source: Beverage Marketing Corporation, personal communication.

A wide range of international water meetings have been held in recent years, from specialized scientific workshops to major international conferences. While it is not clear that these meetings succeed in advancing water solutions,[8] they remain a tool for addressing water-policy challenges and for increasing awareness among stakeholders.

3. Dilemmas

Solving water problems is not easy. While a wide range of technological, economic, and policy responses are available, different approaches succeed and fail in different places. In part, this is the result of a number of dilemmas facing decision makers.

In recent years, one of the most challenging dilemmas has been whether to consider water a public or a private good, and whether public or private models of operation, ownership, and management should be applied.[9] Serious ideological conflicts and disputes have arisen over this issue, with violence in some regions.

The difficulty is that water has the characteristics of both a public and private good and there are advantages and disadvantages of both public and private models for water service. The lack of a clear choice has complicated developing successful and consistent responses to water problems. Some forms of private participation in the delivery of water service cannot be excluded, but limits and guidelines must be set on the role of private entities in providing this public good and service (see Box 1).

Similarly, governments have conflicting priorities for funding and economic development. When capital is limited, as it is in most places, difficult choices must sometimes be made over whether to fund education, water, energy, telecommunications, or other infrastructure developments. While a strong argument can be made that meeting basic human needs for water is one of the fundamental roles and responsibilities of governments, not all governments have acted on those responsibilities.

4. Implications

The failure to address and resolve the policy challenges identified above has a wide range of implications for human health, ecosystem viability, international security, and socio-political equity.

More than 2 million people, and perhaps as many as 5 million, die annually from preventable water-related diseases directly attributable to the failure to meet basic human needs for water.[10] Hundreds of millions of cases of water-related diseases occur annually, with vast economic and social implications for health care, job productivity, the education of children, and more.

Natural ecosystems that depend on hydrologic flows in rivers and streams are increasingly stressed by water withdrawals and use. Many rivers no longer reach their deltas. Fisheries and wetlands are experiencing population declines and loss of function, which ultimately affects human health and economics. Some high-profile ecological disasters include the degradation and extinctions in the Aral Sea, the Colorado River Delta, and the Yellow River. The Aral Sea

Box 1: Principles and Standards for Privatization

Despite significant and often justified opposition to water privatization, proposals for public-private partnerships in water supply and management are likely to become more numerous in the future. There are many forms of water privatization, or public-private partnerships, making unilateral support for, or opposition to, privatization illogical. Gleick *et al.*[11] do not argue that privatization efforts must stop. They do, however, argue that all privatization agreements should meet certain standards and incorporate specific principles. Consequently, this box includes a set of suggested principles and standards for privatization of water-supply systems and infrastructure.

The responsibility for providing water and water services should rest with local communities and governments, and efforts should be made to strengthen the ability of governments to meet water needs. The potential advantages of privatization are often greatest where governments have been weakest and failed to meet basic water needs. Where strong governments are able to provide water services effectively and equitably, the attractions of privatization decrease substantially. Unfortunately, the greatest risks of privatization are also where governments are weakest, where they are unable to provide the oversight and management functions necessary to protect public interests. This contradiction poses the greatest challenge for those who hope to make privatization work successfully.

Continue to Manage Water as a Social Good

Meet basic human needs for water. All residents in a service area should be guaranteed a basic water quantity under any privatization agreement.

Meet basic ecosystem needs for water. Natural ecosystems should be guaranteed a basic water requirement under any privatization agreement.

The basic water requirement for users should be provided at subsidized rates when necessary for reasons of poverty.

Use Sound Economics in Water Management

Water and water services should be provided at fair and reasonable rates.

Whenever possible, link proposed rate increases with agreed-upon improvements in service.

Subsidies, if necessary, should be economically and socially sound.

Private companies should be required to demonstrate that new water-supply projects are less expensive than projects to improve water conservation and water-use efficiency before they are permitted to invest and raise water rates to repay the investment.

Maintain Strong Government Regulation and Oversight

Governments should retain or establish public ownership or control of water sources.

Public agencies and water-service providers should monitor water quality. Governments should define and enforce water-quality laws.

Contracts that lay out the responsibilities of each partner are a prerequisite for the success of any privatization.

Clear dispute-resolution procedures should be developed prior to privatization.

Independent technical assistance and contract review should be standard.

Negotiations over privatization contracts should be open, transparent, and include all affected stakeholders.

has suffered from the overuse of the Amu Darya and Syr Darya rivers for cotton production in Central Asia.

Conflicts over water, particularly subnational conflicts, appear to be on the rise. Table 2 lists a small subset of recent water-related disputes that involved violence, though a far larger number of conflicts are listed in the Water Conflict Chronology, cited earlier. Growing concerns about terrorism have also led water managers to re-evaluate the vulnerability of some systems and to put in place more rapid detection and reporting of problems. A number of the events described in Table 2 fall under the category of terrorism.

5. Future Trajectories/Scenarios

What will the future bring? Many scenarios of future water conditions have been proposed, from the global to the local level.[12] These projections can be optimistic or pessimistic, but few of them are particularly enlightening in terms of how to proceed toward sustainable water management and use. A few scenarios attempt to describe positive visions of the future while still maintaining realistic assumptions about economics, population growth, and the trajectory of technologies.[13]

Most of these share some common characteristics, including improved efficiency of water use, greater efforts to meet basic human and ecological needs for water, improved financing of water development, and perhaps most importantly, better management. Put together, these approaches sketch out a "soft path" for water, defined in recent years by this author and others.[14]

The soft path for water is one that takes advantage of existing centralized infrastructure – the hard path – and complements it by investing in decentralized facilities, efficient technologies and policies, and human capital. The soft path attempts to improve overall productivity of uses rather than to find new sources of supply. It attempts to deliver water services matched to the needs of end users, on both local and community scales. The traditional hard-path approach has produced, and will continue to produce, enormous benefits, such as clean-water supplies, irrigation, and improved human health. But it is also increasingly spawning ecologically damaging, socially intrusive, and capital-intensive projects that fail to deliver their promised benefits,[15] in large part because of the unshakeable, but incorrect, belief of most policy makers that large, centralized water systems are the only way to meet unrelenting growth in demand, and that such demand is an inevitable outcome of growth in population and gross domestic product.

In fact, this is no longer true. Many countries have significantly cut their water use, both total and per capita, by investing in efforts to improve the efficiency of use and reduce waste of water. The United States, for example, uses less water today for all purposes than it did in 1980 – more than twenty-five years ago[16] – despite a much larger economy and population. Figure 1 shows how the "water productivity" in the US has grown over the last few decades.

6. Policy Recommendations

Solutions to water problems exist. The challenge is identifying obstacles to implementation and then overcoming those obstacles. The soft path to water offers a comprehensive set of solutions guided by certain principles:

1. Governments, communities, and private interests should collaborate to meet water-related needs rather than merely to supply water.

2. The productive use of water can be improved by rational application of technology and economics, and by decision making at the right scale.

3. Diplomacy, not violence, must be the principal tool for addressing water conflicts.

4. Ecological health must be considered a fundamental component of water policy.

5. Water decisions must be transparent and help to facilitate equitable apportionment and use.

Standards must also be set for any efforts to develop public-private partnerships for water management. Some efforts have been made in this area (see Box 1) but no set of principles has been universally adopted or implemented. The history of efforts to develop such principles for other water-related problems is mixed. In particular, a multi-year, multi-party effort to develop agreements and principles about the construction and operation of dams – the World Commission on Dams – reached a widely accepted set of principles[17] that have, for the most part, been ignored by governments, marginalized by international funding agencies, and rendered ineffective.

Figure 1: Economic productivity of water in the United States measured in 1996 dollars produced per cubic meter of water withdrawn for all uses. As shown, productivity has almost trebled over the past century due to improvements in water-use efficiency and structural changes in the US economy.

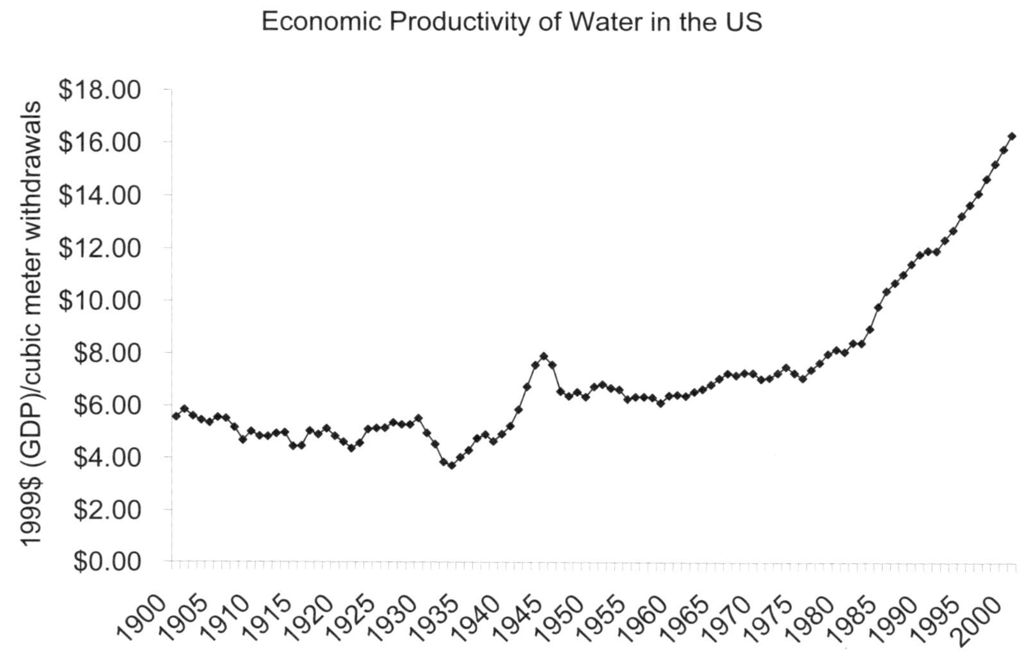

Table 2: Cases From the Water Conflict Chronology, 1990 to 2005, Involving Violence

Source: These examples come from the Water Conflict Chronology of the Pacific Institute, published in *The World's Water* (Washington, DC: Island Press), and periodically updated at http://www.worldwater.org. See the Chronology for a complete set of citations.

Date	Parties Involved	Basis of Conflict	Description
1991-present	Karnataka, Tamil Nadu (India)	Development dispute	Violence erupts when Karnataka rejects an interim order handed down by the Cauvery Waters Tribunal, set up by the Indian Supreme Court. The Tribunal was established in 1990 to settle two decades of dispute between Karnataka and Tamil Nadu over irrigation rights to the Cauvery River.
1991	Iraq, Kuwait, US	Military target	During the Gulf War, Iraq destroys much of Kuwait's desalination capacity during retreat.
1991	Iraq, Turkey, United Nations	Military tool	Discussions are held at the United Nations about using the Ataturk Dam in Turkey to cut off flows of the Euphrates to Iraq.
1991	Iraq, Kuwait, US	Military target	Baghdad's modern water supply and sanitation system are intentionally and unintentionally damaged by the allied coalition. "Four of seven major pumping stations were destroyed, as were 31 municipal water and sewerage facilities – 20 in Baghdad, resulting in sewage pouring into the Tigris. Water purification plants were incapacitated throughout Iraq" (Arbuthnot 2000). In the first eight months of 1991, after Iraq's water infrastructure was damaged by the Persian Gulf War, the *New England Journal of Medicine* reported that nearly 47,000 more children than normal died in Iraq and the country's infant mortality rate doubled to 92.7 per 1,000 live births.
1992	Turkey	Terrorism	Lethal concentrations of potassium cyanide are reported discovered in the water tanks of a Turkish Air Force compound in Istanbul. The Kurdish Workers' Party (PKK) claimed credit.

1992	Bosnia, Bosnian Serbs	Military tool	The Serbian siege of Sarajevo, Bosnia and Herzegovina, includes a cutoff of all electrical power and the water feeding the city from the surrounding mountains. The lack of power cuts the two main pumping stations inside the city despite pledges from Serbian nationalist leaders to United Nations officials that they would not use their control of Sarajevo's utilities as a weapon. Bosnian Serbs take control of water valves regulating flow from wells that provide more than 80 percent of water to Sarajevo; reduced water flow to city is used to "smoke out" Bosnians.
1993	Yugoslavia	Military target and tool	Peruca Dam intentionally destroyed during war.
1995	Ecuador, Peru	Military and political tool	Armed skirmishes arise in part because of disagreement over the control of the headwaters of the Cenepa River. Wolf argues that this is primarily a border dispute simply coinciding with the location of a water resource.
1998	Angola	Military and political tool	In September 1998, fierce fighting between UNITA and Angolan government forces broke out at Gove Dam on the Kunene River for control of the installation.
1998	Democratic Republic of Congo	Military target, Terrorism	Attacks on Inga Dam during efforts to topple President Kabila. Disruption of electricity supplies from Inga Dam and water supplies to Kinshasa.
1998 to 2000	Eritrea and Ethiopia	Military target	Water pumping plants and pipelines in the border town of Adi Quala were destroyed during the civil war between Eritrea and Ethiopia.
1999	Lusaka, Zambia	Terrorism, political tool	Bomb blast destroyed the main water pipeline, cutting off water for the city of Lusaka, population 3 million.
1999	Yugoslavia	Military target	Belgrade reported that NATO planes had targeted a hydroelectric plant during the Kosovo campaign.
1999	Bangladesh	Development dispute, Political tool	50 hurt during strikes called to protest power and water shortages. Protest led by former Prime Minister Begum Khaleda Zia over deterioration of public services and in law and order.
1999	Yugoslavia	Military target	NATO targets utilities and shuts down water supplies in Belgrade. NATO bombs bridges on Danube, disrupting navigation.

1999	Yugoslavia	Political tool	Yugoslavia refuses to clear war debris on Danube (downed bridges) unless financial aid for reconstruction is provided; European countries on Danube fear flooding due to winter ice dams will result. Diplomats decry environmental blackmail.
1999	Kosovo	Political tool	Serbian engineers shut down water system in Pristina prior to occupation by NATO.
1999	South Africa	Terrorism	A homemade bomb was discovered at a water reservoir at Wallmansthal near Pretoria. It was thought to have been meant to sabotage water supplies to farmers.
1999	Angola	Terrorism, political tool	100 bodies were found in four drinking-water wells in central Angola.
1999	China	Development dispute, terrorism	Around the Chinese New Year, farmers from Hebei and Henan Provinces fought over limited water resources. Heavy weapons, including mortars and bombs, were used and nearly 100 villagers were injured. Houses and facilities were damaged and the total loss reached $1 million. Parties involved: Huanglongkou Village, Shexian County, Hebei Province and Gucheng Village, Linzhou City, Henan Province.
1999	East Timor	Military tool, terrorism	Militia opposing East Timor independence kill pro-independence supporters and throw bodies in water well.
1998-1999	Kosovo	Terrorism, political tool	Contamination of water supplies/wells by Serbs disposing of bodies of Kosovar Albanians in local wells. Other reports of Yugoslav federal forces poisoning wells with carcasses and hazardous materials.
2000	Ethiopia	Development dispute	One man stabbed to death during fight over clean water during famine in Ethiopia.
2000	Belgium	Terrorism	In July, workers at the Cellatex chemical plant in northern France dumped 5,000 liters of sulfuric acid into a tributary of the Meuse River when they were denied workers' benefits. A French analyst pointed out that this was the first time "the environment and public health were made hostage in order to exert pressure, an unheard-of situation until now."

2000	Hazarajat, Afghanistan	Development dispute	Violent conflicts broke out over water resources in the villages Burna Legan and Taina Legan, and in other parts of the region, as drought depleted local resources.
2000	India: Gujarat	Development dispute	Water riots reported in some areas of Gujarat to protest authorities' failure to arrange adequate supply of tanker water. Police are reported to have shot into a crowd at Falla village near Jamnagar, resulting in the death of three and injuries to 20 following protests against the diversion of water from the Kankavati dam to Jamnagar town.
2000	Kenya	Development dispute	A clash between villagers and thirsty monkeys left eight monkeys dead and ten villagers wounded. The duel started after water tankers brought water to a drought-stricken area and monkeys desperate for water attacked the villagers.
2000	Australia	Cyber-terrorism	In Queensland, Australia, on April 23, 2000, police arrested a man for using a computer and radio transmitter to take control of the Maroochy Shire wastewater system and release sewage into parks, rivers, and property. This is one of the first documented cases of cyber-terrorism in the water industry.
2000	China	Development dispute	Civil unrest erupted over use and allocation of water from Baiyangdian Lake – the largest natural lake in northern China. Several people died in riots by villagers in July 2000 in Shandong after officials cut off water supplies. In August 2000, six died when officials in the southern province of Guangdong blew up a water channel to prevent a neighboring county from diverting water.
2001	Israel, Palestine	Terrorism, military target	Palestinians destroy water-supply pipelines to West Bank settlement of Yitzhar and to Kibbutz Kisufim. Agbat Jabar refugee camp near Jericho disconnected from its water supply after Palestinians looted and damaged local water pumps. Palestinians accuse Israel of destroying a water cistern, blocking water tanker deliveries, and attacking materials for a wastewater treatment project.
2001	Pakistan	Development dispute, terrorism	Civil unrest over severe water shortages caused by the long-term drought. Protests began in March and April and continued into summer. Riots, four bombs in Karachi (June 13), one death, 12 injuries, 30 arrests. Ethnic conflicts as some groups "accuse the government of favoring the populous Punjab province [over Sindh province] in water distribution."

2001	Macedonia	Terrorism, military target	Water flow to Kumanovo (population 100,000) cut off for 12 days in conflict between ethnic Albanians and Macedonian forces. Valves of Glaznja and Lipkovo Lakes damaged.
2001	China	Development dispute	In an act to protest destruction of fisheries from uncontrolled water pollution, fishermen in northern Jiaxing City, Zhejiang Province, dammed the canal that carries 90 million tons of industrial wastewater per year for 23 days. The wastewater discharge into the neighboring Shengze Town, Jiangsu Province, killed fish and threatened people's health.
2001	Afghanistan	Military target	US forces bombed the hydroelectric facility at Kajaki Dam in Helmand province of Afghanistan, cutting off electricity for the city of Kandahar. The dam itself was apparently not targeted.
2002	Nepal	Terrorism, political tool	The Khumbuwan Liberation Front (KLF) blew up a hydroelectric powerhouse of 250 kilowatts in Bhojpur District on January 26. The power supply to Bhojpur and adjoining areas was cut off. Estimated repair time was six months; repair costs were estimated at 10 million rupees. By June 2002, Maoist rebels had destroyed at least seven micro-hydro projects, as well as an intake of a drinking-water project and pipelines supplying water to Khalanga in western Nepal.
2002	Kashmir, India	Development dispute	Two people were killed and 25 others injured in Kashmir when police fired at a group of villagers clashing over water sharing. The incident took place in Garend village in a dispute over sharing water from an irrigation stream.
2002	Colombia	Terrorism	Colombian rebels in January damaged a gate valve in the dam that supplies most of Bogota's drinking water. Revolutionary Armed Forces of Colombia (FARC) detonated an explosive device planted on a German-made gate valve located inside a tunnel in the Chingaza Dam, which provides most of the capital city's water.
2002	Karnataka, Tamil Nadu, India	Development dispute	Continuing violence over the allocation of the Cauvery River between Karnataka and Tamil Nadu. Riots, property destruction, more than 30 injuries, arrests through September and October.
2003	United States	Terrorism	Four incendiary devices were found in the pumping station of a Michigan water-bottling plant. The Earth Liberation Front (ELF) claimed responsibility, accusing Ice Mountain Water Company of "stealing" water for profit. Ice Mountain is a subsidiary of Nestle Waters.

2003	Colombia	Terrorism, development dispute	A bomb blast at the Cali Drinking Water Treatment Plant killed three workers May 8. The workers were members of a trade union involved in intense negotiations over privatization of the water system.
2003	Iraq, United States, Others	Military Target	During the US-led invasion of Iraq, water systems were reportedly damaged or destroyed by different parties, and major dams were military objectives of the US forces. Damage directly attributable to the war includes vast segments of the water-distribution system and the Baghdad water system, damaged by a missile.
2003	Iraq	Terrorism	Sabotage/bombing of main water pipeline in Baghdad. The sabotage of the water pipeline was the first such strike against Baghdad's water system, city water engineers said. It happened around 7 in the morning, when a blue Volkswagen Passat stopped on an overpass near the Nidaa mosque and an explosive was fired at the 2-meter-wide water main in the northern part of Baghdad, said Hayder Muhammad, the chief engineer for the city's water-treatment plants.
2003-2004	Sudan	Military tool, military target, terrorism	The ongoing civil war in Sudan has included violence against water resources. In 2003, villagers from around Tina said that bombings had destroyed water wells. In Khasan Basao, they alleged that water wells were poisoned. In 2004, wells in Darfur were intentionally contaminated as part of a strategy of harassment against displaced populations.
2004	Mexico	Development dispute	Two Mexican farmers argued for years over water rights to a small spring used to irrigate a small corn plot near the town of Pihuamo. In March, these farmers shot each other dead.
2004	Pakistan	Terrorism	In military action aimed at Islamic terrorists, including Al-Qaida and the Islamic Movement of Uzbekistan, homes, schools, and water wells were damaged and destroyed.
2004	India, Kashmir	Terrorism	Twelve Indian security forces were killed by an IED planted in an underground water pipe during a "counter-insurgency operation in Khanabal area in Anantnag district."
2004	Gaza Strip	Terrorism, development dispute	The United States halts two water development projects as punishment of the Palestinian Authority for their failure to find those responsible for a deadly attack on a US diplomatic convoy in October 2003.

2004	India	Development dispute	Four people were killed in October and more than 30 injured in November in ongoing protests by farmers over allocations of water from the Indira Ghandi Irrigation Canal in Sriganganagar district, which borders Pakistan. A curfew was imposed in the towns of Gharsana, Raola, and Anoopgarh.
2004	Somalia	Development dispute	At least 50 people killed and many more injured in clashes between two divisions of the same clan, in the village of Gelinsor and nearby villages along the Ethiopian border. The fighting reportedly began over access to pastoral land and water wells.
2005	Kenya	Development dispute	Police were sent to the northwestern part of Kenya to control a major violent dispute between Kikuyu and Maasai groups over water. More than 20 people were killed in fighting in January. The tensions arose when Maasai herdsmen accused a local Kikuyu politician of diverting a river to irrigate his farm, depriving downstream livestock. Fighting displaced more than 2,000 villagers and reflects tensions between nomadic and settled communities.

References

[1] World Health Organization, "World Health Report 2003 – Shaping the Future," January 2004, http://www.who.int/whr2001/en/.

[2] United Nations, "The Millennium Goals," United Nations Millennium Declaration A/RES/55/2, September 8, 2000, United Nations, New York.

[3] P.H. Gleick, "Conflict and cooperation over fresh water," in P.H. Gleick (ed.), *The World's Water 1998-1999* (Washington, DC: Island Press, 1998), pp. 105-135; A.T. Wolf, "Water wars and water reality: Conflict and cooperation along international waterways," NATO Advanced Research Workshop on Environmental Change, Adaptation, and Human Security, Budapest, Hungary, October 9-12, 2000.

[4] See www.worldwater.org.

[5] United Nations, *op. cit.*, note 2.

[6] P.H. Gleick, G. Wolff, E.L. Chalecki, and R. Reyes, *The New Economy of Water: The Risks and Benefits of Globalization and Privatization of Fresh Water* (Oakland: Pacific Institute for Studies in Development, Environment, and Security, 2002).

[7] P.H. Gleick, "The myth and reality of bottled water," in P.H. Gleick (ed.), *The World's Water 2004-2005: The Biennial Report on Freshwater Resources*. (Washington, DC: Island Press, 2004), pp. 17-43.

[8] P.H. Gleick, and J. Lane, "Large international water meetings: Time for a reappraisal," *Water International*, Vol. 30, No. 3, 2005, pp. 410-414.

[9] Gleick, *et. al.*, *op. cit.*, note 6.

[10] World Health Organization, *op. cit.*, note 1.

[11] Gleick, *et. al.*, *op. cit.*, note 6.

[12] M.I. L'vovich, *World Water Resources and their Future*, 1979 translation Raymond Nace (ed.) American Geophysical Union, Washington, D.C.; I.A. Shiklomanov, "Assessment of Water Resources and Water Availability in the World," Report for the Comprehensive Assessment of the Freshwater Resources of the World, United Nations, State Hydrological Institute, St. Petersburg, Russia, 1998; P.H. Gleick, "Pictures of the future: A review of global water

resources projections," in P.H. Gleick (ed.), *The World's Water 2000-2001. The Biennial Report on Freshwater Resources* (Washington, DC: Island Press, 2000), pp. 39-61; P.H. Gleick, H. Cooley, D. Groves, *California Water 2030: An Efficient Future* (Oakland: Pacific Institute for Studies in Development, Environment, and Security, 2005).

[13] See for example, P.H. Gleick, *Water 2050: Moving Toward a Sustainable Vision for the Earth's Fresh Water* (Oakland: Pacific Institute for Studies in Development, Environment, and Security, 1997); Gleick, Cooley, Groves, *Ibid*.

[14] See for example P.H. Gleick, "Global freshwater resources: Soft-path solutions for the 21st century," *Science*, Vol. 302, No. 28, November 2003, pp. 1524-1528; O.M. Brandes, and D.B. Brooks, *The Soft Path for Water in a Nutshell* (Victoria: Friends of the Earth, Canada, and the POLIS Project, 2005).

[15] Gleick, *Ibid.*

[16] S.S. Hudson, N.L. Barber, J.F. Kenny, K.S. Linsey, D.S. Lumia, and M.A. Maupin, *Estimated Use of Water in the United States in 2000,* United States Geologic Survey Circular 1268, Reston, Virginia.

[17] World Commission on Dams, Dams and Development: A New Framework for Decision-making, http://www.dams.org.

CHAPTER 17

EDITORIAL OF POLICY BRIEF ON WATER, GLOBALIZATION, AND GLOBAL SECURITY

NAYEF R.F. AL-RODHAN

Dr. Nayef R.F. Al-Rodhan is Senior Scholar in Geostrategy and Director of the Program on the Geopolitical Implications of Globalization and Transnational Security at the Geneva Centre for Security Policy, Geneva, Switzerland

1. Review and Critique

Water is perhaps most frequently viewed in development terms. Yet, it is also a serious and multifaceted security issue. Helga Haftendorn captured very nicely the significance of water to security when she stated that "water is the foundation of human life, is a finite and scarce resource, and is a common and divided resource."[1] Due to its scarcity, its necessity for life and good health, and for sustained development, fresh water is likely to be the source of insecurity, tension, and perhaps conflict in the coming decades. Effectively managing human, economic, and ecosystem demands on water resources, as well as those of various regions that are reliant on a single water basin, constitutes one of the major challenges we face today.[2]

Poor water-quality management can lead to severe health problems. For example, lack of access to clean water, as well as bad sanitation, increases people's vulnerability to water-borne diseases, such as hepatitis A and E and cholera. Moreover, since poor water quality can often lead to diarrhea, inadequate water-quality management can also be an indirect cause of malnutrition. Ill health can, in turn, affect people's capacity to engage in productive economic activity, which can ultimately pose a significant problem for a country's capacity to sustain economic growth. This situation represents a major threat to achieving sustainable development.[3] Thus, inadequate water-quality management and allocation represent a threat not only to human security but also to the economic security of developing countries.

One of the most urgent aspects related to water and globalization that Peter H. Gleick[4] highlights in his policy brief is the failure to meet basic needs for clean water, which results in ill health and death. Ensuring safe, reliable, and reasonably priced water and sanitation presents an ongoing challenge. At present, many people still lack access to clean water and basic sanitation. In addition, the cost-effectiveness of water-quality management policies and activities is poor.

Yet, this represents only part of the problem. As Gleick notes, ecological damage resulting from ineffective water management also presents a major challenge. Water ecosystems are essential both for replenishing and purifying water resources that are vital to health and well-being. Yet, many water ecosystems are suffering from the effects of changes in land use, excessive water withdrawals, as well as contamination as a result of pollution.[5] Thus, there is a dire need to find ways to better support essential ecosystems.

Gleick also identifies the risk of subnational and international violence over shared water resources. The highly publicized dispute between Mexico and the United States over transboundary water management is a case in point.[6] Yet, water conflict is, of course, not limited to this region. In fact, it is increasing in many parts of the world, including the Nile Basin, the Jordan Basin, and the Ganges Basin,[7] often in relation to scarcity or pollution. It can be local, as well as regional. As populations increase, conflicts over the distribution of water resources among different sectors, as well as between different groups, are likely to increase. For instance, conflict may occur over the use of water, e.g., for consumption, irrigation, and power generation. Conflict may also arise as a result of lack of access to freshwater resources, caused either by an inequitable distribution of water resources or absolute scarcity.

2. Dilemmas and Our Recommendations

Globalization presents both opportunities and challenges for water management. Developing successful strategies to effectively manage shared water resources is particularly difficult given conflicting interests among various actors, as well as diverse models for water management, insufficient understanding of the risks and benefits of globalization, and varying state institutional capacities around the world. We highlight eight dilemmas related to this issue and eight corresponding recommendations that may contribute to appropriate policy choices.

Since water scarcity and pollution are among the contributing factors of water conflict, governments face the difficult task of balancing increased water use as a result of economic development against the amplified need for water conservation and desalination technologies, which are costly ventures. We suggest that one way to deal with this problem is to encourage transnational technological innovation and cooperation in order to meet growing global demand for water through desalination of seawater. The huge costs involved in large-scale water projects, such as desalination, as well as the construction of dams, is simply unaffordable for many low-income states. Investments by multinationals and governments, provided that there is sufficient governmental oversight, offers a solution to this problem.

Another major challenge facing states and international organizations is to ensure access to clean water, as well as its quality. We suggest that governments, along with international organizations, should increase their commitment to ensuring that water meets adequate health standards. In order to minimize conflicts related to the use of water, governments also need to think seriously about how to avoid depletion and dependence on underground water resources. In our view, policy makers should prevent the use of underground water for large-scale agriculture and restrict its use for human consumption.

An additional issue that governments face is meeting water-acquisition needs, given the high cost of water transportation. This problem is particularly acute in developing countries, where a great deal of the population is unlikely to have the financial means to acquire water at high prices. A potential solution to this policy problem is to develop the political, economic, and security regulations with which to transport and distribute water at an affordable price.

Finally, some states are confronted with the difficulty of managing both subnational and international conflicts over shared water. In order to prevent both substate and international conflicts over water, states should view water as a basic human need and, as such, as an essential dimension of human security. States must transcend narrow economic and political self-interests in order to better provide for the security of their populations, as well as to avoid conflicts.

3. Conclusion

While normally perceived as a development and health issue, water is also an important security issue. Since it forms the foundation of human life, is scarce, and is a common resource, water can lead to ill health, death, lack of economic growth, as well as subnational and international conflicts if it is badly managed. We should, therefore, conceive of water management as an essential tool in the provision of human, societal, economic, and transnational security. Our aim has been to highlight some of the issues that need to be resolved in relation to water management, as well as to propose potential solutions to the problems facing governments in this area.

References

[1] H. Haftendorn, "Water and International Conflict," paper presented at the 40th Annual Convention of the International Studies Association, Washington, DC, February 16-20, 1999, p.1.
[2] The Economic and Development Review Committee, Organization for Economic Cooperation and Development, *Improving Water Management: Recent OECD Experience* (OECD, 2003).
[3] *Ibid.*
[4] For the brief in its entirety, please see Chapter 16.
[5] For further information, see the World Health Organization's website: http://www.who.int/heli/risks/water/water/en/index.html. Also see the World Health Organization's report "Ecosystems and Human Well-being: A Health Synthesis," 2005, available at http://www.who.int/globalchange/ecosystems/ecosystems05/en/index.html.
[6] A. Peshard-Sverdrup and M. Bishop, "U.S.-Mexico Transboundary Water Management: The Case of the Rio Grande/Rio Bravo: Recommendations for Policymakers for the Medium and Long Term," Center for Strategic and International Studies, January 2003.
[7] Haftendorn, *op. cit.*, note 1.

CHAPTER 18

NATURAL DISASTERS, GLOBALIZATION, AND THE
IMPLICATIONS FOR GLOBAL SECURITY

EMILY MUNRO

Ms. Emily Munro is Training and Academic Affairs Coordinator at the Geneva Centre for Security Policy, Geneva, Switzerland

Abstract
Natural disasters seem to be occurring with greater frequency, and, although perhaps mitigated by improved early-warning mechanisms, a number of large-scale natural disasters in the past three years have served to highlight the human costs and global consequences of natural events. The tsunami in the Indian Ocean, the earthquake in Pakistan, and Hurricane Katrina in the United States affected individuals across national boundaries and required a transnational response. This policy brief will look first at the human-security challenges posed by natural disasters and the complex coordinated national and international responses they require and then at the impact these disasters have on global security and the relationship between natural disasters and globalization.

1. Introduction

The impact of, and response to, recent natural disasters illustrate the two tendencies of recent security thinking: that is, the move up from the *state* to the *global* level and below to the *individual* and to concerns for human security.[1] Natural disasters affect individuals at the most basic level, killing or injuring them, destroying homes and livelihoods and disrupting access to health services, clean water, and adequate housing. These effects create extreme and often prolonged insecurity for those concerned. On the other hand, natural disasters impact not only one nation-state but often an entire region and beyond (e.g., global financial markets), and they also require a coordinated international response from multiple actors. Globalization has made the impact of natural disasters more complex and, it can be argued, has also facilitated a more coordinated response because of the inherent interconnectedness of actors.

The tsunami in the Indian Ocean, the earthquake in Pakistan, and Hurricane Katrina are distinctive events that were particular to the regions they impacted (i.e., developed vs. less developed), the extent of the destruction and damage, and the progress of the response and recovery efforts to date. However, these three events illustrate important commonalities about the impact of, and response to, natural disasters and may help us understand the interplay of these events with the behavior of key actors in the context of globalization.

The Indian Ocean tsunami devastated large parts of South and Southeast Asia after an earthquake off the coast of Indonesia precipitated a large tsunami that hit land on December 26, 2004, with almost no advance warning to coastal populations. The death-toll figures are astounding: 160,000 in Indonesia, 31,000 in Sri Lanka, 10,000 in India, and 5,000 in Thailand, with more deaths in the Maldives and even as far away as Somalia.[2] A total of 12 countries were affected. Beyond the death figures, the number of people who were missing, displaced (1.6 million[3]) suffered injuries, lost their homes and/or jobs is in the millions.

On October 8, 2005, an earthquake measuring 7.6 on the Richter scale rocked Pakistan (and North India and Afghanistan), causing 80,000 deaths and having an impact on 3 million others.[4] As with the tsunami, the effects on the people, local infrastructure, and the economy were enormous and will be felt for decades to follow.

Unlike the tsunami and the earthquake in Pakistan, Hurricane Katrina's impact was experienced by a global power and one of the most developed countries in the world, the United States (US). Despite, or perhaps because of, this, the lessons that can be drawn from the problems caused by, and the response to, this hurricane are important. In terms of figures, Hurricane Katrina forced 770,000 people to leave their homes and 1,300 people lost their lives after the hurricane hit the Gulf Coast in August 2005.[5]

There has been an upsurge in the number and worldwide impact of natural disasters in recent years. Statistics compiled by the United Nations' International Strategy for Disaster Reduction (ISDR) point toward an alarming trend. For example, in the period 1950-59, the ISDR recorded 291 natural disasters, while from 1990 through 1999, 2,711 natural disasters were recorded.[6] In particular, floods and tidal waves, storms, droughts and related disasters, and landslides and avalanches have increased at a disproportional rate.

In the next two sections, I will look at the policy challenges and responses to the tsunami, the earthquake in Pakistan, and Hurricane Katrina from the human-security angle and at how the responses were coordinated. Following this, and from a more macro-level, this paper will address some of the broader dilemmas in responding to natural disasters and the relationship between these events and global security and globalization. Finally, recommendations on how to improve the response to future natural disasters will be presented.

2. The Fundamental Policy Challenge Posed by Natural Disasters: The Impact on Human Security

Natural disasters almost by definition impact individuals first. When a natural disaster – be it a tornado or a massive earthquake – strikes, people's livelihoods and ability to continue with day-to-day life are affected immediately, whether directly or indirectly.

The populations in the affected areas of the earthquake in Pakistan, the Indian Ocean tsunami, and Hurricane Katrina had to grapple with a complex host of attacks on their ability to lead their normal lives. In the first two cases, this was complicated by acute levels of poverty and underdevelopment and in some instances conflict. The following sectors presented the local and international communities with a complex range of policy challenges and the need for urgent but requisite responses:

> *Housing:* Often, the most immediate effect of a natural disaster is the destruction of, or severe damage to, housing. For instance, Hurricanes Rita and Katrina combined led to the destruction of 300,000 houses and damage to 1.85 million others.[7] According to United Nations (UN) estimates, in Pakistan 203,579 housing units were destroyed and another 196,574 were damaged.[8] In tsunami-affected areas, a major problem was the reestablishment of land boundaries, something that delays the rebuilding of new homes or leads to possible legal disputes at a later date.

Internal displacement: A corollary to the destruction of housing, internal displacement leads to a sense of despair and the need for the local authorities and international organizations working in these areas to establish temporary housing and humanitarian assistance rapidly. This was complicated in Pakistan by the onset of winter conditions in the high mountain regions where the earthquake hit, necessitating winterized tents and heavy blankets – the so-called Winter Race by the UN. Relatives and friends host disaster victims, often adding additional economic strains. Displacement problems are complex and long-lasting: one year after the tsunami, the United Nations Office for the Coordination of Humanitarian Affairs (OCHA) estimated that 1 million people were still displaced.[9] In the southern United States, traffic jams blocked transportation routes as people moved inland, with some stuck as the hurricane hit land – a total of 770,000 people were forced to move to other parts of the United States.[10] Given the speed at which people must move, family separation often occurs.[11]

Health care: Health services are often severely disrupted during natural disasters. Even when some health services are available, access can be severely restricted. For those injured during a disaster, this is an immediate problem. The earthquake in Pakistan destroyed or severely damaged over 70 percent of health facilities.[12] In Aceh, Indonesia, the Australian development agency is assisting in the rebuilding of a provincial hospital where they found that 1 in 10 hospital staff was either dead or missing as a result of the tsunami.[13] During Hurricane Katrina, hospitals were put under considerable strain, back-up generators were relied upon, and urgent surgeries were postponed.[14]

Psychosocial effects: The trauma caused by natural disasters should not be underestimated, and psychological support is needed following disasters in the short and long term. The World Health Organization (WHO) has been active in addressing mental-health concerns both in tsunami-affected countries and in Pakistan following the earthquake.[15] A recent statistical analysis of the perception of Hurricane Katrina on the population addresses how people who did not evacuate (42 percent) versus those who did (58 percent) experienced the storm.[16]

Vulnerable groups (women, children, elderly, disabled, poor): Certain groups are more vulnerable when a natural disaster occurs.[17] For instance, elderly people were particularly affected during Hurricane Katrina, and charges of racial discrimination were quickly leveled at government authorities after a slow response to the hurricane.[18] In Pakistan, it was noted that a large proportion of deaths occurred among women and children.[19]

In addition to the sectors mentioned, other problems such as damage to infrastructure and the overall disruption to people's ability to carry on with their jobs produce increased insecurity. Thus, all told, the insecurity brought to bear on populations experiencing natural disasters is enormous and enduring. The response to these disasters, discussed in the next section, focuses on how the range of actors involved work together to provide immediate humanitarian assistance to meet basic human needs and in the medium to long term move the focus to sustainable reconstruction and efforts to mitigate the impact of future natural disasters.

3. Local and International Responses to Natural Disasters

The policy challenges presented by natural disasters require immediate responses combined with long-term planning for sustainable strategies for returning the affected areas to more secure conditions. The first response will be to treat the most pressing humanitarian concerns: treating injured survivors, supplying food and temporary housing, establishing the extent of the damage, addressing the worst-affected areas, and dealing with the large-scale devastation to transportation and other essential infrastructure. Coordination of the response is a key factor in how the challenges of handling a disaster are met.

Hurricane Katrina illustrated flaws in the United States' approach to responding to natural disasters. The federal response was led by the Federal Emergency Management Agency (FEMA). The US Senate recommended in April 2006 that FEMA be dismantled as a result of its poor performance during Katrina. State and local authorities in the US have the primary responsibility of responding to natural disasters, but, given the magnitude of the impact of Katrina, they were unable to cope, and all levels of government (federal, state, and local) needed to be fully involved. Due to the inadequacies of the national response and depth of destruction, the US Peace Corps was involved in disaster relief on US territory for the first time. International support was also required.[20] A key disappointment was the inefficient coordination and decision making and the lack of effectiveness of the various actors.

The earthquake in Pakistan was the first disaster that used a new "cluster" approach, which assigned various UN and other organizations a sector, e.g., the International Organization for Migration (IOM) led the housing sector.[21] The entire operation was led by the OCHA, which was represented by a UN humanitarian coordinator and supported by a UN Disaster Assessment and Coordination Team. Daily cooperation was handled by the UN Disaster Management Team. The Government of Pakistan immediately established a Federal Relief Commission to coordinate its activities. Levels of financial support have been mixed with $5.8 billion in pledges being promised at a donor conference in mid-November 2005 and a further $4 billion in loans, but not all of this has been received.

The response to the tsunami was complicated by the enormous area and number of countries requiring assistance, but the needs of the 12 affected countries varied. For example, Indonesia, especially Aceh, was by far the worst affected, and some countries, including India, said that they did not need external assistance. In Indonesia, a Multi-Donor Trust Fund was established to pool incoming funds. As one of the major donor blocs, the European Union (EU), has stated: "coordinating the recovery programmes has been a major challenge, and has taken place at different levels."[22] Several conferences bringing together relevant actors have taken place across the region to reflect on the best practices and lessons learned.[23] The OCHA's role was, as in Pakistan, essential as the coordinating body, establishing a Tsunami Task Force and chairing the Inter-Agency Standing Committee on the disaster, as well as acting as a key liaison with UN member states.[24]

The response to the all three disasters required a high level of coordination among all the actors providing relief. Common elements include:

- The need for one coordinating body at the national (federal government) or international level (UN);[25]

- Clarification of the roles of non-governmental organizations (NGOs) and local actors; and

- Effective processing of pledged funding and sustained funding.[26]

The coordination of the immediate emergency assistance and even of the more medium- to long-term reconstruction strategies does not address the underlying need to understand and develop a plan to mitigate the impact of future disasters. According to an NGO working on natural disasters, these schemes can often be inexpensive and effective.[27] Examples of these types of projects include, in Pakistan, the establishment of building standards for earthquake-resistant structures and a large-scale project in the Indian Ocean for a tsunami warning system;[28] or, in Indonesia, having better land-tenure records available to validate title and facilitate reconstruction.

4. Related Dilemmas in Responding to Natural Disasters

Natural disasters occur in a social and political context, not just in a physical environment. This influences the impact of natural disasters, complicates relief and reconstruction efforts, and affects long-term recovery. Some of these areas include:

> *Environment:* Natural disasters often have a tremendous impact on the environment, which makes communities more vulnerable to other disasters in the future. For example, the tsunami devastated coral-reef systems, mangroves, and wetlands, which exposed vulnerabilities.[29] As M. Dillon argues, in the context of a discussion on the globalization of security, natural catastrophes will have social and political consequences that "can engender or compound natural ones."[30] A fictional book, *State of Fear*, by well-known author Michael Crichton, suggests that public concerns over global warming have grown, inappropriately, in response to the manipulations of some environmentalists who point to purely natural disasters as evidence of human activity on climate.

Crichton's claims have not been taken very seriously in scientific and academic circles.

Development: As noted above, certain groups are more likely to be affected by natural disasters. This includes the impoverished, as was demonstrated in all three of the disasters addressed here. Low levels of development in Pakistan and experience from other relief operations has led to a call for a "pro-poor" focus to disaster relief, given that this group is especially "disadvantaged in recovery, by limited access to resources, and fewer options for recovery,"[31] as well as to a call to guarantee that efforts are made to not only bring affected populations to pre-disaster development levels but to "ensure that households are restored to better living conditions" than before.[32]

International media coverage and attention: Relief efforts in the wake of natural disasters rely on external funding from countries, the private sector, and individuals. The longevity of media coverage of a particular disaster is largely dependent on the magnitude of the disaster, thereby increasing compassion and competition with other major news stories. The tsunami occurred during the Christmas holiday season in the West, thereby likely leading to an increase in donations. Hurricane Katrina led to an outpouring of sympathy from Americans toward their fellow citizens.

Economics: Natural disasters have widespread economic consequences for individuals, countries, and regions. The reduction in the supply of energy that followed Hurricane Katrina, for instance, has led American observers to warn of risks to energy and economic security.[33] Reduced tourism in tsunami-affected areas led to losses of revenue in Thailand, for example.

Therefore, it is clear that natural disasters have an impact not only on one or two areas but increasingly have widespread consequences for a variety of sectors and over a wide geographic area.

5. The Implications for Global Security and Globalization

The three natural disasters presented here were large in scale, high in impact, and extensive in terms of the damage inflicted. Thus far, the focus has been on the human insecurities created by these disasters, the coordinated response required to address the complex policy challenges engendered by the disasters, and additional dilemmas that presented themselves. However, the impact of these disasters has also been felt beyond the individual and community level by countries, regions, and the global system. The implications for future disaster relief and response operations can be learned from these experiences:

1. *Widespread human impact:* Foreign nationals vacationing across the Indian Ocean were affected by the tsunami, especially in Thailand and Sri Lanka; many foreigners lost their lives. The Pakistani diaspora living around the world searched for information on their families and friends affected by the earthquake. Without globalization and the increased migration of people for economic reasons and for tourism around the world, these natural disasters would not have been felt as broadly outside of the immediately affected areas.

2. *Multiplicity of actors and ease of information exchange:* As demonstrated above, these three natural disasters required a complex response from a range of different actors, from the governments of the countries affected (local authorities, as well as at the state, regional, and federal levels) to local and international NGOs and international organizations. Globalization has made information much more readily available, especially with the use of the Internet, and therefore international assistance was more easily generated and should have been better able to reach those most directly in need. The coordination of these actors, although far from perfect, as discussed above, was made easier by extensive national and international mechanisms already in existence to respond to disasters.

3. *Conflict:* In the case of the tsunami, the disaster impacted two regions in conflict: Aceh in Indonesia and Sri Lanka. In the former, the tsunami had a demonstrably positive effect on

forging peace: "the humanitarian emergency triggered by the tsunami provided a critical opportunity for change in Aceh – prying open the province... and offering an avenue for ending the conflict."[34] A peace deal was signed on August 15, 2005, that is still holding up. In Sri Lanka, the tsunami did not provide such an opening, and peace talks recently stalled, and there has been an increase in hostilities. In the earthquake zone of northern Pakistan, Kashmir was also affected, and India and Pakistan have cooperated to reach victims; however, no broader steps to diminish the conflict have been taken.[35] Unfortunately, no parallels can be drawn with the "earthquake diplomacy" that took place after a large earthquake struck Turkey in 1999 that resulted in an amelioration of relations with Greece.[36]

4. *Geopolitics:* Although international organizations, especially the United Nations, play a central role in coordinating relief efforts, it is states that provide the overwhelming majority of the funding. The tsunami relief effort provides an interesting case study of power and natural-disaster assistance, whereby we saw the Australian government play a central role in Southeast Asia (especially Indonesia), followed by the US, Japan, India, and Singapore.[37] It is interesting that China was limited in its response to the disaster[38] and India sought to send a strong message of its growing power, stating that it did not need external support. The foreign military presence of the US and Australia made the Indonesian government especially nervous. In the case of Hurricane Katrina, international support, however limited, was provided to the United States to complement domestic relief efforts.

Natural disasters impact security at various levels from the individual to the global, and our response to future disasters must take into account these realities. Disasters do not occur within strict national boundaries, their effects can be felt across the world, and responses must be broad and comprehensive. Security no longer refers only to state security or the absence of conflict; it also includes individual and environmental security and global health concerns. Global security and globalization help to ensure that large-scale natural disasters do not occur in isolation; therefore, responses must be equally coordinated and take into account broadening security concepts.

6. Policy Recommendations

The following recommendations aim to influence how local and international actors respond to natural disasters, taking into account the widespread impact and influence of the destruction and damage caused by disasters from the human to global levels, all the while recognizing the important steps already being taken by these actors in fashioning innovative and effective responses.

1. Responses to natural disasters must give primacy to human-security concerns throughout the entire relief and reconstruction effort (short and long term), with a special emphasis on vulnerable groups such as women. International organizations and NGOs involved in relief and reconstruction following natural disasters should ensure that individual security is mainstreamed throughout all programming.

2. Local ownership and involvement in natural-disaster relief and reconstruction must be assured. National and subnational actors, governmental and non-governmental, should be represented on coordinating bodies organizing the response to natural disasters. The international community must recognize the importance of listening and responding to local concerns from the beginning of relief efforts.

3. Relief and reconstruction activities are most effective for a region when they aim to increase the region's long-term prospects for higher levels of development and disaster preparedness. In addition, development programs in natural-disaster-prone areas (e.g. earthquake zones) can include specific activities to increase awareness and preparedness for these unpredictable events, e.g., public information campaigns and encouragement and financial support for better construction practices.

4. The environmental consequences of natural disasters should be addressed with the aim of reducing the environmental

strains caused by disasters and the effect they have on communities.

5. Research into why there has been a dramatic increase in the number and frequency of natural disasters should be supported with the aim of reducing the future impact of such disasters and developing comprehensive policies for handling this increase.

6. Opportunities for having a positive impact on existing conflict situations in disaster-affected regions should be fully exploited in a timely manner. In the wake of a natural disaster, there is sometimes an opportunity to resolve or at least have a positive influence on an existing conflict. External actors must exploit these opportunities, however small they may seem.

7. The now global impact of natural disasters must be recognized, and efforts to limit the widespread negative (human, political, or economic) effects of disasters should be identified. These could include the establishment of reliable mechanisms to find information on missing family members and the establishment, to the extent possible, of better protection for critical infrastructure, such as ports and oil platforms, to minimize longer-term economic impacts.

References

[1] R. Thakur, "Human Security: Incoherent Concept or Policy Template," speech delivered at the Bonn International Centre for Conversion, March 9, 2006, http://www.bicc.de/events/vortraege_2006/thakur.php.

[2] A. Bardalai, "In the Tsunami's Wake," *National Interest*, Spring 2005, pp. 108-112.

[3] "Back to Work: How People are Recovering their Livelihoods 12 months after the Tsunami," Oxfam International, Oxfam Briefing Paper, December 20, 2005, p. 2.

[4] "Starting On the Road to Recovery: Saving Lives and Rebuilding Livelihoods After the Pakistan Earthquake," Oxfam International, Briefing Note, January 29, 2006, p. 1. The IOM estimates that 70,000 will be left severely disabled. "Update on IOM Operations: South Asia Earthquake – Pakistan," International Organization for Migration, p. 2.

[5] Statement by Homeland Security Secretary Michael Chertoff before the Senate Committee on Homeland Security and Governmental Affairs, February 15, 2006; "Special Report: Recovering States? The Gulf Coast Six Months After the Storms," Oxfam International, Oxfam Briefing Paper, February 2006.

[6] "Disaster Statistics 1994-2004," United Nations/International Strategy for Disaster Reduction, http://www.unisdr.org/disaster-statistics/introduction.htm.

[7] Oxfam, *op. cit.*, note 5, p. 10.

[8] "Pakistan 2005 Earthquake: Early Recovery Framework," United Nations System, Islamabad, Pakistan, November 2005, p. 14.
[9] "Coordination and the Indian Ocean Tsunami." OCHA in 2006: Activities and Extra-budgetary Funding Requirements, http://ochaonline.un.org/ocha2006/chap6_1.htm.
[10] Chertoff, *op. cit.*, note 5.
[11] See, for example, http://www.familylinks.icrc.org/katrina.
[12] Oxfam, *op. cit.*, note 4, p. 11.
[13] "Australia's Response to the Indian Ocean Tsunami: Report for the Period Ending 30 November 2005," AusAID, Australian Government, p. 5.
[14] Also see S. Dewan, "Evacuee Study Finds Declining Health," *The New York Times*, April 18, 2006.
[15] See "Tsunami Wreaks Mental Health Havoc," *Bulletin of the WHO*, Vol. 83, No. 6, June 1, 2005, http://www.who.int/bulletin/volumes/83/6/infocus0605/en/index.html; Post Disaster Mental Health Relief Programme of the Ministry of Health of Pakistan and the WHO, outlined at http://www.whopak.org/pdf/Post%20Disaster%20Mental%20Health%20Relief.pdf.
[16] "Hurricane Katrina: Perceptions of the Affected," Fritz Institute, April 2006, http://www.reliefweb.int/library/documents/2006/fin-gen-26apr.pdf.
[17] As Oxfam has stated, natural disasters "are profoundly discriminatory. Wherever they hit, pre-existing structures and social conditions determine how a community will be affected and who will pay the highest price." Oxfam, *op. cit.*, note 5, p. 6.
[18] The southern US states are also some of the poorest states in the United States.
[19] United Nations System, *op. cit.*, note 8, p. 10. In general, also see L. Chew and K.N. Ramdas, "Caught in the Storm: The Impact of Natural Disasters on Women," The Global Fund for Women, December 2005. It was reported that, in Pakistan, 500 children were killed in one school. "Don't be Scared, be Prepared: How Disaster Preparedness can Save Lives and Money," Christian Aid, December 2005.
[20] A confidential ICRC report outlining logistical coordination failures has been made public, http://www.nytimes.com/packages/pdf/national/20060404_arc_missionreport.pdf.
[21] United Nations System, *op. cit.*, note 8, pp. 2-6. Initial lessons from this cluster approach have begun to be drawn, such as the need to define cluster activities better and to try to include all actors operating in the field in a cluster.
[22] "The EU's Contribution to the International Response to the 2004 Asian Tsunami: Achievements, Next Steps and Lessons Learned," Department for International Development, United Kingdom and European Commission, Discussion Paper, Brussels, December 20, 2005, p. 7.
[23] See the reports from the following workshops: "National Post-Tsunami Lessons Learned and Best Practices Workshop," June 8-9, 2005, Government of Sri Lanka and United Nations, Colombo, Sri Lanka; "National Workshop on Tsunami Lessons Learned and Best Practices in Thailand," Government of Thailand and United Nations, Bangkok, May 30-31, 2005; "Regional Workshop on Lessons-Learned and Best Practices in the Response to the Indian Ocean Tsunami," United Nations, Medan, Indonesia, June 13-14, 2005.
[24] United Nations System, *op. cit.*, note 8.
[25] See, on this aspect, "Strengthening Emergency Relief, Rehabilitation, Reconstruction, Recovery and Prevention in the Aftermath of the Indian Ocean Tsunami Disaster," Economic and Social Council, General Assembly, United Nations, June 21, 2005.
[26] See "Predictable Funding for Humanitarian Emergencies: A Challenge to Donors," Oxfam International, Briefing Note, October 24, 2005. The private sector has become an important donor to relief efforts: for the tsunami alone, the US private sector donated $360 million (and possibly in the end $700 million). "Going the Distance: The US Tsunami Relief Effort 2005," US Department of State, p. 7, http://usinfo.state.gov/products/pubs/tsunami/tsunami.pdf.
[27] Christian Aid, *op. cit.*, note 19.
[28] Oxfam, *op. cit.*, note 4, p. 8; "Indian Ocean Tsunami Warning System by mid-2006," *New Scientist*, January 20, 2005.

[29] Bardalai, *op. cit.*, note 2. For an analysis of the environmental impact of the earthquake in Pakistan, see "An Assessment of Environmental Risks and Needs: Earthquake in Pakistan," World Conservation Union, January 16, 2006.

[30] M. Dillon, "Global Security in the 21st Century: Circulation, Complexity and Contingency," in ISP/NSC Briefing Paper 05/02, "The Globalization of Security," Chatham House October 2005, p. 3.

[31] T. Beck, "South Asia Earthquake 2005: Learning from Previous Recovery Operation," ALNAP and Provention Consortium.

[32] Oxfam, *op. cit.*, note 4, p. 4.

[33] F. Verrastro, "Energy Policy Considerations in the Aftermath of Hurricane Katrina," Center for Strategic and International Studies, remarks made for the Arab-US Policymakers Conference, September 12, 2005; E. Chow and J. Elkind, "Hurricane Katrina and US Energy Security," *Survival*, Vol. 47, No. 4, Winter 2005-06, pp. 145-160.

[34] "Natural Disasters and Peacemaking: Aceh: Peacemaking after the Tsunami," Worldwatch Institute, http://www.worldwatch.org/features/disasters/aceh-1, adapted from M. Renner and Z. Chafe, "Turning Disasters Into Peacemaking Opportunities," in Worldwatch Institute, *State of the World 2006* (New York: W.W. Norton & Co., 2006). Also see the International Crisis Group's work on the peace in Aceh.

[35] M. Renner, "Peacemaking in Kashmir: From Physical Tremor to Political Earthquake?," Worldwatch Institute, Global Security Brief No. 8, December 6, 2005, http://www.worldwatch.org/features/security/briefs/8/.

[36] D. Keridis, "Earthquakes, Diplomacy, and New Thinking in Foreign Policy," *The Fletcher Forum of World Affairs*, Vol. 30, No.1, Winter 2006, pp. 207-214.

[37] T. Huxley, "The Tsunami and Security: Asia's 9/11?," *Survival*, Vol. 47, No. 1, Spring 2005, pp. 123-132.

[38] *Ibid.*, p. 127.

CHAPTER 19

EDITORIAL OF POLICY BRIEF ON NATURAL DISASTERS, GLOBALIZATION, AND THE IMPLICATIONS FOR GLOBAL SECURITY

NAYEF R.F. AL-RODHAN

Dr. Nayef R.F. Al-Rodhan is Senior Scholar in Geostrategy and Director of the Program on the Geopolitical Implications of Globalization and Transnational Security at the Geneva Centre for Security Policy, Geneva, Switzerland

1. Review and Critique

The impact of natural disasters, such as the tsunami in the Indian Ocean, the earthquake in Pakistan, and Hurricane Katrina in the United States (US), is relevant to both human and transnational security. Natural disasters affect individuals at the most fundamental level, injuring or killing them, leaving them homeless, displacing them, destroying their livelihoods, as well as disrupting health-care services, clean water supplies, and adequate housing facilities. Moreover, particular segments of the population may be disproportionately affected by natural disasters.[1] Women, children, the elderly, the disabled, and the poor may be particularly exposed to the effects of natural disasters.

As Emily Munro points out in her policy brief,[2] natural disasters can also make communities more vulnerable in the future by, for example, devastating or disrupting local ecosystems. In addition, at the state level, the damage to infrastructure, as well as the disruption to productive activity, can pose significant economic problems. Natural disasters take an enormous toll on development. They can even put at risk some countries' very capacity for development. Sometimes, however, natural disasters are the result of regrettable development strategies. The development choices made by individuals, communities, and states can increase the risks related to natural disasters, as well as distribution thereof among the population of affected countries. Buildings that collapse during earthquakes and bridges that are washed away by floods were all, at some point, integral parts of development projects.

Disasters can also interact with and exacerbate other problems, such as furthering the spread of disease, worsening substate conflict, damaging the environment, and increasing migration. Many of these problems are not confined to individual states but are transnational in nature. An effective disaster-relief strategy is, thus, often transnational or multilateral. Cooperative disaster-relief efforts can, in some instances, even help to ease tense relations or actual conflict situations. For example, Greek-Turkish relations improved slightly following the 1999 earthquakes.[3] Cooperative disaster preparedness could even form part of conflict-prevention initiatives.

Both human and economic vulnerability to natural disasters can be reduced if effective disaster-management strategies are put in place. Such strategies require quick and coordinated responses from an array of actors. Globalization has implications for the impact of natural disasters and may encourage more coordinated responses to them. Since disaster response depends to a large degree on external funding from various countries, the private sector, non-governmental organizations (NGOs), and individuals, globalization may help to facilitate the mobilization of resources. Increased access to the media, for example, may sensitize a greater number of people nationally, as well as internationally, to the scale and impact of any given natural disaster and thereby encourage donations to relief efforts.

2. Dilemmas and Our Recommendations

Developing successful strategies that enable local and international actors to effectively respond to natural disasters is vital to increasing human, economic, and transnational security. We highlight eight dilemmas related to this issue and eight corresponding recommendations that may contribute to appropriate policy choices.

Natural disasters affect the individual first, injuring and killing, as well as removing the necessary conditions for people to provide for their basic needs. In other words, natural disasters affect human security in the first instance. Yet, many policy makers are accustomed to thinking in terms of national security. Thus, states face the challenge of reconciling human and national security.

In our view, human security should be given priority within the context of national security. It is only by prioritizing the individual that states will respond to natural disasters in a timely, well-organized, and impartial way.

Lack of preparedness for natural disasters is not just confined to developing countries. As Hurricane Katrina has demonstrated, developed countries also need to improve their capacities in this area. All policy makers, therefore, need to focus on developing capabilities for maximum preparedness for natural disasters, and they also need to avoid underestimating the effects of disasters, especially in poorer regions of the world. In order to be more prepared, states need to establish better early-warning systems. Ideally, this would involve transnational analysis of potential disasters, as well as better and more effective formulation of transnational scenarios and solutions. Existing early-warning systems should also be strengthened.

For large-scale natural disasters, multinational, coordinated responses are likely to be part of an effective disaster response. While it may seem self-evident that dealing with the fallout of natural disasters requires transnational relief efforts, some states may perceive outside intervention with suspicion. Therefore, it is crucial that transparent and coordinated multilateral relief avoid real or perceived ulterior, geopolitical motives for assistance. United Nations (UN) monitoring and logistical support may also serve to alleviate suspicions about external interventions.

States also face the problem of balancing the need for sophisticated civil defense systems to manage disasters with investing in a system that is aimed at managing infrequent events. We suggest that extensive training and preparedness should be maintained, because the expense of not doing so is likely to exceed the cost of prevention. Adequate preparedness will also require simulations to be carried out by states and international organizations to ensure that relief is delivered to the most vulnerable. Failure to do so may result in uneven disaster relief.

3. Conclusion

While we are accustomed to conceiving of natural disasters as environmental or humanitarian issues, they also constitute important security concerns. Specifically, they represent significant threats to human and economic security. While globalization can contribute to the severity of natural disasters by contributing to, for instance, global warming, it may also have some positive spin-offs for disaster-response efforts. It can facilitate the prediction of natural disasters, raise immediate aid contributions and post-disaster funds through media coverage, and encourage cooperation between different actors.

References

[1] See P. Hough, *Understanding Global Security* (London and New York: Routledge, 2004), Ch. 8.
[2] For the brief in its entirety, please see Chapter 18.
[3] United Nations Development Programme, Bureau for Crisis Prevention and Recovery, "Reducing Disaster Risk: A Challenge for Development," New York, 2004, p. 73.

CHAPTER 20

CHANGING HEALTH PARADIGMS, GLOBALIZATION, AND GLOBAL SECURITY

BATES GILL
XIAOQING LU

Dr. Bates Gill is Freeman Chair in China Studies at the Center for Strategic and International Studies, Washington, DC, United States

Ms. Xiaoqing Lu is Research Associate with the Freeman Chair in China Studies at the Center for Strategic and International Studies, Washington, DC, United States

Abstract
Globalization is a double-edged sword. The emergence in recent years of major ongoing and potential health threats, coupled with the globalizing nature of international affairs, compels us to take health as a serious global security issue. But globalization also creates opportunities for greater collaboration and synergy at the regional and global levels.
In light of the policy challenges and responses of major governments and the international community, it is clear that the world continues to face fundamental dilemmas in terms of organization, resources, and capacities to fight health-related challenges. Failure to generate necessary political and financial support to meet the challenges of global health threats has serious security implications. A far greater sense of urgency will be needed from political leaders and the prioritization they give to health and the impact it has on stability, security, and prosperity. Perhaps most importantly, the international community needs to seriously consider how it is organized to combat transnational health challenges.

1. Policy Challenges

The world is confronting a growing list of emerging transnational threats to global security. Paradoxically, the very benefits of globalization – the increasing integration of economies around the world, and the ever-freer flow of goods, capital, people, and information across international borders – also help strengthen and facilitate the spread of new transnational threats. A short list of such transnational challenges in the current era would include weapons proliferation, terrorism, environmental degradation, organized crime, the movement of displaced persons, and trafficking in humans, drugs, and contraband.

However, while these critical challenges have received the considerable attention they deserve from the international community, the security threats posed by global health challenges have received far less. Traditionally, health problems have not been seen as security problems. They have been seen predominantly as the purview of national authorities and not of transnational import, and a country-by-country approach has been taken to dealing with them. However, the emergence and reemergence in recent years of existing and potential health threats, coupled with the globalizing nature of international affairs, compels us to take health as a serious global security issue.

Hundreds of millions of people face serious health threats. Since 1945, three diseases alone – HIV/AIDS, tuberculosis, and malaria – have claimed 150 million lives.[1] Each year, these three infectious diseases kill over 6 million people worldwide, and the number is still growing.[2] Meanwhile, non-communicable diseases are another major cause of death, leading to 35 million deaths worldwide in 2005 alone.[3]

The devastating effects of HIV/AIDS in Africa provide a stark example. With just over 10 percent of the world's population, sub-Saharan Africa, the region hardest hit by the disease, is home to two-thirds of all people living with HIV/AIDS, or approximately 25.8 million people. An estimated 2.4 million adults and children died of HIV-related illnesses in this region in 2005, while a further 3.2 million people became newly infected.[4] According to the United Nations Joint Program on HIV/AIDS (UNAIDS), the disease has now infected roughly 50 million Africans since the early 1980s, of whom more than 22 million have died.

The impacts of the epidemic are manifold. Life expectancy has fallen by more than a decade in many African countries and is now likely below 40 years in the hardest-hit areas. HIV/AIDS has orphaned 12 million African children and in some countries every sixth child has lost at least one parent to the disease.[5] The World Bank estimates that every minute four young people (aged 15 to 24) become infected with HIV/AIDS in Africa.

Besides the drastic human loss, the spread of the disease also threatens to compromise socioeconomic and democratic gains in the region. HIV/AIDS often has the greatest impact on productive members of society in the prime of life. Thus, the prevalence of HIV/AIDS diminishes agricultural and health workforces, increasing food insecurity and burdens of health care in society. Statistics from the United Nations indicate that the epidemic is already pushing Africa in the wrong direction and retarding progress toward meeting the Millennium Development Goals, including eradicating extreme poverty and hunger, combating HIV/AIDS, reducing child mortality, and improving maternal health. Specifically, 23 sub-Saharan countries are failing in half or more of the goals, while merely 10 countries are currently on track to meet half the goals or more.[6]

Institutions that provide national and regional military security in Africa are endangered as well, which creates a vacuum for gangs and terrorist organizations to fill. Military personnel, peacekeepers, and peace observers rank consistently among the groups most affected by HIV/AIDS, often with infection rates two to three times that of the local population.[7] Evidence is accumulating that HIV/AIDS has the potential to hamper any attempt at building a secure and stable community in the region.

Another case in point is the potential global outbreak of avian flu. Since 1997, when the first human contracted H5N1 in Hong Kong, the disease has spread across Asia to the Middle East, Europe, and Africa, with the prospect that it might also spread to the Americas and elsewhere. As of mid-2006, H5N1 had killed some 127 people, and over 200 million poultry had died of the disease or had been culled.[8] Historical evidence demonstrates that flu pandemics have occurred cyclically over past centuries, roughly between every 30 and 50 years. In this sense, the world is "overdue" for another flu pandemic.[9]

Without effective and prompt detection and containment, the spread of a pandemic flu could result in significant human casualties and catastrophic socioeconomic consequences, potentially threatening regional and global prosperity and security.[10] Due to the limited supply of existing vaccines and other prevention and treatment resources, divisive global competition will likely ensue in the presence of a worldwide disease outbreak, putting human and regional security at the greatest risk. Moreover, as seen in the case of the outbreak of severe acute respiratory syndrome (SARS) in 2003, our intensely globalized world provides an excellent vehicle for the rapid spread of such pathogenic viruses to all corners of the Earth.

Other emerging and reemerging diseases – such as malaria, tuberculosis, schistosomiasis, dengue fever, West Nile virus, or highly pathogenic viruses such as the Ebola virus – can have similarly destabilizing consequences, especially in resource-poor environments.

2. Responses

The link between public health and security has slowly gained greater attention in recent years. Convinced that the prevalence of HIV/AIDS is reaching catastrophic dimensions, the Clinton administration for the first time formally identified the disease as a threat to United States (US) national security in 2000. The 2000 US National Intelligence Estimate recognized that new and re-emerging infectious diseases would pose a rising global health threat and would complicate US and global security over the coming decades.

The Estimate pointed out that "these diseases would endanger U.S. citizens at home and abroad, threaten U.S. armed forces deployed overseas, and exacerbate social and political instability in key countries and regions in which the United States has significant interests."[11] In January 2003, President George W. Bush announced a $15 billion, five-year initiative to fight the epidemic abroad, named the President's Emergency Plan for AIDS Relief (PEPFAR).

Shortly after this announcement, the director of the US Central Intelligence Agency, in a statement on worldwide threats, said that "the national security dimension of the virus [HIV] is plain: it can undermine economic growth, exacerbate social tensions, diminish military preparedness, create huge social welfare costs, and further weaken already beleaguered states. And the virus respects no border."[12]

The European Union (EU) has also stepped up its efforts by addressing health problems as a security challenge. The EU-US Declaration on HIV/AIDS, Malaria and Tuberculosis in 2004 claimed that "the spread of communicable diseases is one of the biggest threats to human life, prosperity and security."[13] Japanese leaders have also begun to adopt new ways of looking at security, particularly human security. Acknowledging that good health is an essential factor for security, the Japanese government pledged $265 million to the Global Fund to Fight AIDS, Tuberculosis and Malaria.[14]

The World Health Organization (WHO) is at the forefront of global efforts to combat diseases, and increasingly recognizes the linkage between security and health. The WHO has mobilized considerable resources to tackle serious diseases such as smallpox, polio, leprosy, cholera, and tuberculosis over the past fifty years. But with a static yearly budget of $1 billion, and operating within the benefits and limits of the United Nations system, the WHO is constrained from fully confronting the transnational health challenges we face.[15]

Meanwhile, the Global Fund to Fight AIDS, Tuberculosis and Malaria was established to dramatically increase resources to fight three of the world's most devastating diseases. A partnership among governments, civil society, the private sector, and affected communities, the Global Fund has committed $4.9 billion in 131 countries to support aggressive intervention programs.[16] The Global Fund represents an innovative and accountable approach to address common global issues. Nevertheless, it still struggles with a widening gap between donor countries' pledges and the actual amount committed to the Global Fund.

However, in spite of these important acknowledgements of the health-stability linkage, and the introduction of innovative international efforts to combat global health threats, far greater political and financial commitment is needed. The commitment must come not only from relevant health authorities, but also from key security, economic, development, and military policy communities. In short, a more comprehensive and global response is needed in the face of the comprehensive and global challenges we face.

3. Dilemmas

In light of these policy challenges and the response of the international community to them so far, it is clear that the world continues to face fundamental dilemmas.

First, with each passing day, the nature of the international system becomes all the more globalized, challenging traditional ways of thinking and organizing to combat security threats. The transnational spread of disease is no exception. But by and large, the international community's approach to battling health threats today remains wedded to state-centric models that prioritize borders and state sovereignty. The structural mismatch between globalized threats and state-centered mindsets hinders well-coordinated and effective responses to those threats.

A second dilemma lies in the sheer scarcity of resources – political, financial, material, and human – to address growing global health concerns. Despite mounting attention given to the issue of public health, it is still not a top priority on the international political and budgetary agenda. Health agencies and organizations are typically weak bureaucratic actors with dwindling budgets, facing shortages of funding and operative authority. Other, better-funded agencies, such as in the security sector, do not see health-related matters as part of their mission.

The sustained lack of political and financial commitment translates into continued and in some cases widening deficiencies in terms of material and human capacity. Throughout the developing world, while the expert community often knows "what works" in the way of prevention, treatment, and care, there is simply a lack of the necessary tools – from vaccinations, to mosquito nets, to medicines – to adequately prevent and treat disease. Even where necessary interventions are available, many parts of the world lack the needed trained personnel to administer them effectively. In other cases, the complexity of emergent health threats – such as HIV/AIDS or the H5N1 virus – stays ahead of the international expert community, defying satisfactory scientific and medical solutions.

4. Implications

Failure to generate necessary political and financial support to meet the challenges of global health has serious security implications. Health problems will continue to threaten nation-states, especially poor states where there is serious lack of resources and infrastructure for prevention and treatment programs to take root. HIV/AIDS, SARS, and other infectious diseases disrupt social and economic systems and undermine political stability, especially in poorer, more vulnerable states.

Yet, developed countries have a high stake as well. The transnational spread of diseases underscores the shared fate of the developed and developing worlds. The World Bank estimates that a potential influenza pandemic could cost the global economy up to $800 billion and reduce the world's gross domestic product by 2 percent.[17] To combat major health crises at home, developed countries will have to divert support from other pressing issues on the international front, such as counterterrorism, scientific and medical research, poverty alleviation, and environmental protection.

5. Future Trajectories

The 2006 Report on the Global AIDS Epidemic released by UNAIDS estimates that around 38.6 million people were living with HIV/AIDS worldwide in 2005, with 4.1 million people newly infected in 2005 alone. As new infections mount, it is clear that we are not winning the global battle against the epidemic. HIV/AIDS continues to advance around the world at an alarming pace. As the US National Intelligence Council estimated in 2002, the "next wave" of the epidemic would be driven by the spread of HIV/AIDS in five populous countries – Nigeria, Ethiopia, Russia, India, and China – where the number of infected people will grow from around 14-23 million currently to an estimated 50-75 million by 2010.[18]

In many Asian countries, HIV/AIDS will be spread initially through the sharing of dirty needles by heroin addicts, a highly efficient method of disease transmission. But prevention, treatment, and care interventions in the drug-shooting populations are exceedingly complex, complicating effective measures to combat the further spread of HIV.

Emerging from Asia, avian influenza has quickly crossed borders to many countries in the Middle East, Europe, and Africa, with the prospect that it might also spread to the Americas and elsewhere. With a looming human pandemic, the world community will be tested on its ability to pull together with strong political will and determination. The resurgence of other diseases, such as tuberculosis and malaria, is also on the horizon. As the environment continues to deteriorate, environment-related health problems have also started to emerge.

6. Policy Recommendations

Globalization is a double-edged sword. We recognize the health challenges that globalization can accelerate. But globalization also creates opportunities for greater collaboration and synergy at regional and global levels. Several key recommendations include:

1. A far greater sense of urgency will be needed from political leaders and the prioritization they give to health and the impact it has on stability, security, and prosperity.

Leading members of the international community will need to speak out far more forcefully about the threats posed by health-related challenges, not only in terms of human suffering, but also in terms of national, regional, and global security. Major actors in the international system should empower executive-branch special envoys to formulate policy and mobilize resources to address looming health challenges, and to do so with a far more comprehensive mandate encompassing prevention, treatment, care, development, and security.

2. Greater financial commitments should be made and implemented at the international, national, and local levels.

Higher political priority will hopefully translate into greater financial, material, and capacity-building resources on the ground. In addition to alleviating suffering and stemming social and economic instabilities, these resources will also need to target human capacity building – from medical care to project-management expertise and oversight – in order to build a larger and sustainable international reserve of health-related talent. Leaders need to begin thinking now how to close funding and resource gaps at the Global Fund and the WHO, and to sustain the future of PEPFAR beyond its current initial commitment of five years.

3. National governments and the international community should be better organized to achieve broader integration and more effective utilization of resources.

Perhaps most importantly, the international community needs to seriously consider how it is organized to combat transnational health challenges. Looking to organizations such as UNAIDS and the Global Fund, similarly collaborative, multidimensional organizations – which draw together the resources of a broad range of institutions and organizations – will be needed to face future challenges such as an avian flu pandemic. In particular, international and national governments will need to more fully integrate the talent and resources of the private sector, such as civil society organizations and the business community. In addition, these organizations, both those in existence and in the future, will also need to integrate their work more closely with national and international security-related players such as national militaries, law enforcement, and international peacekeepers.

The enormous problems posed by HIV/AIDS – a disease first diagnosed more than two decades ago – have at last compelled the international community to think and organize more effectively, resulting in higher political commitments, greater resources, and smarter response mechanisms. And yet, as the grim progression of HIV/AIDS and its devastating effects demonstrate, we still fall far short of what is needed. The lessons from this tragedy should force us all to take steps now to mobilize commitments, resources, and organizations to better head off the next major health threat to global and regional security.

References

[1] World Health Organization (WHO), "Removing Obstacles to Healthy Development, Report on Infectious Diseases," 1999, accessed online at http://www.who.int/infectious-disease-report/.
[2] The Global Fund to Fight AIDS, Tuberculosis and Malaria website, http://www.theglobalfund.org/en/.
[3] WHO, World Health Statistics 2006, accessed online at http://www.who.int/whosis/whostat2006.pdf.
[4] UNAIDS and WHO, "AIDS Epidemic Update December 2005," accessed online at http://www.unaids.org/epi/2005/doc/EPIupdate2005_pdf_en/epi-update2005_en.pdf.
[5] World Bank, "HIV/AIDS Regional Update – Africa," accessed online at http://web.worldbank.org/WBSITE/EXTERNAL/COUNTRIES/AFRICAEXT/EXTAFRHEANUTPOP/EXTAFRREGTOPHIVAIDS/0,,contentMDK:20415756~menuPK:1830800~pagePK:34004173~piPK:34003707~theSitePK:717148,00.html.
[6] UNDP and UNICEF, *The Millennium Development Goals in Africa: Promises & Progress* (New York, 2002.)
[7] M. Schneider and M. Moodie, "CSIS HIV/AIDS Taskforce Report: The Destabilizing Impacts of HIV/AIDS," accessed online at http://www.csis.org/media/csis/pubs/0205_destimp.pdf.
[8] WHO, "Cumulative Number of Confirmed Human Cases of Avian Influenza," May 29, 2006, accessed online at http://www.who.int/csr/disease/avian_influenza/country/cases_table_2006_05_29/en/index.html.
[9] T. Salaam-Blyther and E. Chanlett-Avery, "U.S. and International Responses to the Global Spread of Avian Flu: Issues for Congress," Congressional Research Service (CRS), January 9, 2006.
[10] B. Gill, testimony before the Congressional-Executive Commission in China, February 24, 2006, "China's Response to Avian Flu: Steps Taken, Challenges Remaining, and Transparency," accessed online at http://www.cecc.gov/pages/roundtables/2006/20060224/Gill.php.
[11] National Intelligence Council, "The Global Infectious Disease Threat and Its Implications for the United States," NIE-99-17D, January 2000, accessed online at http://www.cia.gov/cia/reports/nie/report/nie99-17d.html.
[12] G. Tenet, Director of Central Intelligence's Worldwide Threat Briefing, "The Worldwide Threat in 2003: Evolving Dangers in a Complex World," February 11, 2003, accessed online at http://www.cia.gov/cia/public_affairs/speeches/2003/dci_speech_02112003.html.

[13] The White House, Office of the Press Secretary, "E.U.-U.S. Declaration on HIV/AIDS, Malaria and Tuberculosis," June 26, 2004, accessed online at http://www.state.gov/p/eur/rls/fs/36893.htm.

[14] Asia Society, "The Human Security Challenges of HIV/AIDS and Other Communicable Diseases: Exploring Effective Regional and Global Responses," March 22, 2004, accessed online at http://www.asiasource.org/asip/HIV_Japan.pdf.

[15] BBC, "World Health Organization: A Profile," April 25, 2003, accessed online at http://news.bbc.co.uk/2/hi/health/2975139.stm.

[16] The Global Fund to Fight AIDS, Tuberculosis and Malaria, *op. cit.*, note 2.

[17] BBC, "1.9 Billion Pledged for Bird Flu Fight," January 18, 2006, accessed at http://news.bbc.co.uk/go/pr/fr/-/1/hi/world/asia-pacific/4622982.stm.

[18] National Intelligence Council, "The Next Wave of HIV/AIDS: Nigeria, Ethiopia, Russia, India, and China," ICA 2002-04 D, September 2002, accessed online at http://www.odci.gov/nic.

CHAPTER 21

EDITORIAL OF POLICY BRIEF ON CHANGING HEALTH PARADIGMS, GLOBALIZATION, AND GLOBAL SECURITY

NAYEF R.F. AL-RODHAN

Dr. Nayef R.F. Al-Rodhan is Senior Scholar in Geostrategy and Director of the Program on the Geopolitical Implications of Globalization and Transnational Security at the Geneva Centre for Security Policy, Geneva, Switzerland

1. Review and Critique

Health is not immediately perceived as a security issue. Yet, as Jared Diamond points out in his book *Guns, Germs, and Steel*, health issues have long been central to determining our fate.[1] Indeed, recent potential health threats, particularly within the context of increased transnationalization of food production, travel, and migration, force us to think of health as a paramount security concern. As Bates Gill and Xiaoqing Lu note, the impact of epidemics such as HIV/AIDS has been devastating. For example, HIV/AIDS is currently eroding Africa's already fragile development capacities. HIV/AIDS is also looming large over India's promising potential.[2] The emergence of new diseases such as HIV/AIDS has also been accompanied by the re-emergence of old ones such as tuberculosis and malaria. The statistics speak for themselves: in 2005, 3 million people died of AIDS-related illness, 5 million were newly infected with HIV, and 3 million people were killed by malaria and tuberculosis.[3]

Yet, unlike other transnational threats to security, such as organized crime and terrorism, health risks have failed to generate the same sense of urgency, with perhaps the exception of avian influenza, to which states were quick to respond. As Gill and Lu indicate in their brief, part of the problem lies in the fact that health-care issues are traditionally conceived of as domestic concerns to be dealt with by individual national authorities.[4] Yet, threats posed by diseases tend to be transnational in nature and require a significant degree of cooperation between states.

Moreover, the capacity to respond effectively to health issues depends on the existence of an adequate and widely accessible health-care system, as well as on well-managed scarce resources. In fact, according to the World Health Organization (WHO), part of the reason for the catastrophic proportions of the HIV/AIDS epidemic in sub-Saharan Africa is the number of failed states in that region.[5] Failed states are unlikely to respond effectively to health issues, many of which are transnational in nature. Limited state capacities, often due to funding gaps, can prevent the establishment, as well as reform, of health-care systems, in many areas of the world. Even political upheaval on a less dramatic scale leads to threats to health security. One of the effects of the arduous transition from communism in Russia, for instance, has been the rise of vaccine-preventable diseases, such as tuberculosis and diphtheria.[6]

The world continues to face fundamental dilemmas in terms of organization, resources, and capacities to fight health-related challenges. Failure to generate necessary political and financial support to meet the challenges of global health concerns has serious security implications. While it can facilitate the spread of sickness, it can also offer unprecedented opportunities to mobilize the resources with which to improve the overall health of humankind. Policy makers should make it an imperative to reduce the negative health implications of globalization and to draw on the possibilities that globalization offers with regard to reducing health insecurity.

2. Dilemmas and Our Recommendations

Thus, health issues present states with a number of challenges. Health care and surveillance of emerging diseases need to be thought of as transnational and not simply national concerns. Improving health or human security, however, implies not only cooperation between states but also greater solidarity between rich and poor states. We identify eight dilemmas related to health and security, as well as eight corresponding recommendations that we hope will contribute to the debate.

The major challenge facing policy makers is to reformulate the health paradigm in such a way as to reflect the transnational nature of many threats to health. Equally important is raising global awareness about transnational health threats through, for example, education. Preventative measures, as well as adequate intervention tools, should also be improved. Along with states, international and non-governmental organizations are likely to play a central role in sensitizing people to the often global dimensions of health risks.

A significant dilemma is posed by the existence of transnational health threats within a world of sovereign states. The existence of state sovereignty makes enforcement measures extremely difficult. As a result, disease-control requirements are as yet not enforceable. Governments ought to negotiate a multilateral treaty on general disease control. This should be accompanied by disease- and region-specific protocols, as well as the sharing of best practices.

Another factor aggravating states' ability to effectively address health concerns is increased pressure on states to reduce public funding for health-care provision within the context of intensified economic competition. In order to ameliorate this situation, transnational health threats should be identified as challenges to both security and stability. States should also devote more resources to eliminating the causes of infectious diseases. Failed or failing states should be assisted in meeting established global health-care standards. The linkage between health and economic security, particularly in developing states, ought to be made. In many countries, structural adjustment and neo-liberal health-sector reforms are hampering developing states' ability to improve the health of their populations. In our view, the commercialization of health-care systems should be reviewed and debts should be cancelled.

Effective governance capacities should be encouraged within these states and partly funded through increased donor assistance. Best practices and technology should also be shared with them.

A large part of health insecurity is connected with the cost of medicines and the subsequent lack of, or inconsistent, treatment. The dilemma is in reconciling the short-term profit incentives of pharmaceutical companies with the need for increased accessibility of the poor to essential medicines. In order to help alleviate this problem, the duration of patents on new medicines should be reviewed. Increased availability of generic medicines should also be ensured. Incentives for investments in the development of vaccines and medicines should also be promoted.

3. Conclusion

Thus, health is central not only to human security but also to state security and stability. States should therefore devote adequate resources to improving health care. They should also address the underlying causes of sickness. Since many health-care problems are transnational in nature, states also need to adapt state-centric health paradigms and to cooperate actively with other states to prevent and halt the spread of infectious diseases.

References

[1] J. Diamond, *Guns, Germs, and Steel* (London and New York: W.W. Norton and Company, 1997).
[2] P. Mitra and T.C. Schaffer, "Public Health and International Security: The Case of India," available online at http://www.csis.org/media/csis/pubs/060731_aids_india.pdf.
[3] "The Global Fund to Fight AIDS, Tuberculosis and Malaria, 2005 Annual Report," available online at http://www.theglobalfund.org/en/files/publications/annualreport2005/.
[4] For the brief in its entirety, please see Chapter 20.
[5] WHO, "The World Health Report 2006: Working Together for Health," available at http://www.who.int/whr/2006/en/.
[6] P. Hough, *Understanding Global Security* (London and New York: Routledge, 2004), p. 159.

CHAPTER 22

US ENVIRONMENTAL POLICY AND GLOBAL SECURITY

JENNIFER WALLACE

Ms. Jennifer Wallace is Course Coordinator for the International Training Course in Security Policy at the Geneva Centre for Security Policy, Geneva, Switzerland

Abstract
There are direct linkages that bind environmental damage and degradation to matters of global security, whether defined in the traditional sense of the "hard" security of the state or the broader category of "human" security, which includes the physical well-being and economic security of the individual. Environmental damage itself covers an enormous array of challenges: climate change, water and air pollution, and ozone depletion, to name a few. National policies are insufficient to fully address environmental damage, which is a supranational concern that transcends borders and includes the quality of the "common goods" of the Earth's water and air. The challenge is thus to find global mechanisms, supported at the national level, that prevent, reverse, or prepare for the effects of environmental change. The role and policy of the United States is a logical place to focus on how such challenges are being addressed; most importantly because the influence of the United States on and within the international community is such that the priority given to environmental issues is a barometer of the global impact of policy responses. The often competing interests of the domestic environmental lobby with the industrial business lobby, which often finds itself in opposition to environmental regulations and limits on toxic chemicals, can be seen as a battle of long-term security versus short-term economic interests, the outcome of which has global implications both in setting priorities on the national and international policy agenda and for the direct environmental impacts of resulting policies.

1. Policy Challenges

There are direct linkages that bind environmental damage and degradation to matters of global security, whether defined in the traditional sense of the "hard" security of the state or the broader category of "human" security, which includes the physical well-being and economic security of the individual.[1] Environmental damage itself covers an enormous array of challenges: climate change, water and air pollution, and ozone depletion, to name a few. The threat to human security is perhaps the more apparent: disease caused by a contaminated water supply or skin cancer that is a result of ozone depletion are obvious examples of threat to the individual. Global warming can also potentially lead to destructive weather patterns that lead to crop failure and starvation, or cataclysmic events that indiscriminately threaten national security. Although the linkages to climate change are debated, Hurricane Katrina, which struck the United States (US) in 2005, is considered by many experts to be at least in part the result of global warming,[2] and resulted in the deaths of nearly 1,500 people and displaced over 1.5 million. In addition, the linkages of environmental damage to matters of traditional state security are also real. The protection and destruction of the water supply, for example, has been associated with conflict for centuries. Water has factored into modern-era warfare as well, notably in the Arab-Israeli War of 1967, with control of the tributaries of the Jordan River, or in a 1990 crisis when Turkey blocked the flow of the Euphrates to fill its own reservoir.[3] Crop failures and water shortages caused by global warming or contamination can also lead to refugee flows, as well as to both internal and transborder conflicts.

Complicating the issue is the complexity of identifying and addressing the root causes of environmental degradation or damage, which include both natural (and likely irreversible or uncontrollable) trends; those caused by man through lack of alternatives, ignorance, or indifference (such as pollution); and, in the so-called age of terror in particular, the concern of intentional acts of contamination or destruction of resources. Even the root challenges of natural shifts in the environment can be disputed at the national and international level; for example, the scientific evidence linking carbon dioxide emissions and other greenhouse gases to global climate change is not uncontested. Such disagreements present real challenges to effective implementation of safeguards, which require a cooperative international response. National policies are insufficient to fully address environmental destruction, which is a supranational concern that transcends borders and includes the quality of the "common goods" of the Earth's water and air. The challenge is thus to find global mechanisms, supported at the national level, that prevent, reverse, or prepare for the effects of environmental change.

The role and policy of the United States is a logical place to focus on how such challenges are being addressed for a variety of reasons. Most importantly, the influence of the United States on and within the international community is such that the priority given to environmental issues is a barometer of the global impact of related policy responses. In addition, the United States is one of the largest net contributors of carbon dioxide emissions,[4] which has been linked to global climate change, although the correlation is still debated by skeptics, including some in the Bush administration.[5] Carbon dioxide emissions are also one of the more troubling causes of environmental damage (as well as resource depletion via consumption of fossil fuels) that can be directly linked to human actions that can be regulated, as opposed to naturally occurring environmental shifts or acts of terrorism. Furthermore, the United States has one of the strongest environmental lobbies, consisting of numerous, well-funded non-governmental organizations (NGOs) that enjoy strong grassroots support.[6] The often competing interests of the environmental lobby with the industrial business lobby, which mostly opposes environmental regulations and limits on toxic chemicals,[7] can be seen as a battle of long-term security versus short-term economic interests, the outcome of which has global implications both in setting priorities on the national and international policy agenda and for the direct environmental impacts of resulting policies.

2. Responses

Primarily due to interests that compete with that of addressing environmental threats or providing environmental security, the policy response of the United States and particularly that of the current Bush administration can at best be seen as temperate. While the list below is not a fully comprehensive list of policy responses, due the numerous pieces of legislation passed since environmental policy took a more substantive place in national political discourse in the late 1960s, it includes the major proposals that guide current US environmental discourse and shape international environmental policy. The legislation and US government programs and policies that are currently in effect include the following:

The *National Environmental Policy Act of 1969* (NEPA), signed by President Richard Nixon and still the effective guidelines for federal environmental regulation, has the following stated purpose: "To declare a national policy which will encourage productive and enjoyable harmony between man and his environment; to provide efforts which will prevent or eliminate damage to the environment and biosphere and stimulate the health and welfare of man; to enrich the understanding of the ecological systems and natural resources important to the Nation; and to establish a Council on Environmental Quality."[8] The act requires federal programs and agencies to provide an environmental impact assessment before undertaking any major project.

The *Environmental Protection Agency* (EPA), the federal body devoted to environmental safeguards, was established in 1969 under NEPA. This agency's mission is "to protect human health and to safeguard the natural environment," through research, assessments and policies.[9] The agency administers laws directly and via state governments. Federal legislation enforced by the EPA includes: the Clean Air Act of 1970; Clean Water Act of 1972; Safe Drinking Water Act of 1974; Resource Conservation and Recovery Act of 1976; Toxic Substance Control Act of 1976; Energy Policy and Conservation Act of 1978; Comprehensive Environmental Response, Compensation and Liability Act of 1980 (Superfund); Asbestos Hazard Emergency Responses Act of 1986; and Oil Pollution Act of 1990.

Nonetheless, as a federal agency, the neutrality and independence of the EPA in carrying out its mandate has been questioned, with particular criticism aimed at industry-sponsored testing to determine chemical restrictions. Many in the EPA acknowledge this criticism, but cite lack of funds for the failure to conduct independent assessments.

Another relevant policy response of the US government, albeit a negative one vis-à-vis environmental protection, is its *failure to ratify the Kyoto Protocol,* or the legally binding addendum to the United Nations (UN) Framework Convention on Climate Change. The Bush administration cited the Protocol's weaker standards toward developing nations, economic concerns, and lack of scientific proof as the primary reasons for the withdrawal of the United States from negotiations.[10]

3. Dilemmas

The global threats caused by environmental damage and degradation, including, *inter alia,* human-security threats, resource-based conflicts, and population shifts, must be mitigated through international cooperation. This initiative faces the following dilemmas:

At the national political level:

- How can the priority of environmental concerns be elevated on the US policy agenda, particularly given the influence of competing interests, such as the industrial business lobby?

- How can national policy makers (elected officials), whose personal short-term interests include reelection, be convinced to support potentially unpopular measures (e.g., increased taxation of fuel) to make decisions in support of long-term environmental protection?

At the international political level:

- How can cooperative measures be established that involve both widespread international support and specific, goal-oriented, and enforceable actions, thereby resulting in effective implementation?

At the conceptual level:

- Can environmental destruction, and especially global climate change, be traced to its root causes, so that common and scientifically based criteria on which to base national legislation and international agreements can be established?

4. Implications

- If national legislators (elected officials) are to increase their commitment to environmental safeguards, they require *public support*. The public will thus need to see environmental protection as a core value and accept the negative trade-offs associated with protection, such as increased regulation, higher taxes on fuel and other scarce or toxic substances, financial commitments to research and enforcement bodies, etc.

- At the international level, the United States and other countries must reach common and measurable agreements and accept supranational authority that measures and enforces compliance. The entrance into such binding international agreements is a commitment that implies some degree of a loss of sovereignty,[11] which must be made acceptable to the United States through political pressure on the national government from both the domestic population and the international community. The goal of such pressure for international compliance should be the establishment of a *clear, unbiased and transparent enforcement body* that can be supported by the United States.

- In order to create an environment of international cooperation, in which effective common action is possible, support *for the specific needs of developing countries* must be addressed. Countries that struggle economically typically must prioritize the attraction and support of industry to combat joblessness, even under conditions that are environmentally hazardous. If developing countries are thus expected to meet similar levels of compliance as developed nations, then support for the economies of developing countries must be forthcoming in the form of aid and investment, so that poverty and economic hardship do not replace environmental threats as causes of human insecurity.

- The implications above, which include public awareness and increased political attention, are facilitated by *complete and accurate information* on the causes and consequences of environmental damage. Research and experimentation, such as the search for alternative energy options to cut carbon dioxide emissions, must be encouraged and financially supported. While exact scientific evidence is not strictly required to implement precautionary environmental safeguards, increased awareness of the causes and effects of environmental damage would help focus the international community, and the national governments that comprise it, on specific and effective steps to address the issue.

5. Future Trajectories/Scenarios

Environmental damage compounds over time and can eventually lead to conditions that affect health or survival, and/or situations of desperation (e.g., for food, water, resources, etc.) that can lead to violent conflict. Specifically, rising temperatures can reduce access to water, which may also lead to the spread of disease. Particularly in developing countries that are ill-equipped to manage such a crisis, there could be a movement of "environmental refugees" from resource-scarce areas.[12]

Currently, it is predicted that the "rise in temperature under most forecasts over the next 15 years is unlikely to lead to significant physical disruptions—such as major rise in sea level or alteration of agricultural production—therefore, physical changes to the world's climate are likely to have only a negligible impact on bilateral relations by the end of the next decade."[13]

Nonetheless, average surface temperatures of the Earth have risen over the past century, so the greenhouse effect will remain a significant policy issue. Political pressure on governments to take constructive action to combat global warming is expected to increase in case of future cataclysmic weather-related events, such as Hurricane Katrina, despite an unclear causal relationship.[14]

States that presently accrue income from depleting natural resources, particularly Middle East countries whose economies are based on oil wealth, may face increasing levels of instability unless alternative sources of revenue are found. Regardless of the quantity of fossil fuels remaining, the rent-based states may face a crisis as alternative sources of energy are discovered and developed.

Related to this, a Chatham House/National Intelligence Council (NIC) study asserts that the global climate change will necessitate a "reconsideration of the role of nuclear power, multiply non-proliferation and waste management issues, induce rising water levels and temperature change that impact on coastal populations and agricultural production."[15]

The NIC identifies a dilemma for policy makers in identifying future effective economic safeguards, asserting that "an environmental regime based solely on economic incentives will probably not produce needed technological advances because firms will be hesitant to invest in research when there is great uncertainty about potential profits. On the other hand, a regime based on government regulations will tend to be costly and inflexible."[16]

US leadership and participation will be key to the successful implementation of any initiatives, both as a key emitter of pollutants and as a major political power that can provide funding, expertise, and global influence if it sets environmental protection as one of its core values.

6. Policy Recommendations

The US government should adopt the following policy recommendations in order to more effectively address the global threat caused by environmental damage:

1. The United States must *make a real commitment and targeted efforts to seek alternative sources of energy to reduce its dependence on fossil fuels.* First, this would provide energy independence and allow US disengagement from Middle Eastern mineral-rich countries that will likely become more volatile as resources deplete. Furthermore, new energy sources will likely reduce the levels of air pollution currently caused by carbon dioxide emissions from burning fossil fuels.

2. *Domestic economic policies (taxation/subsidization) should be tailored to encourage the use of cleaner forms of energy.* The state and federal tax burden on gasoline has not changed significantly since 1991, averaging around 41 cents per gallon.[17] Increases in taxes on fossil-fuel consumption, as well as subsidies for the purchase of hybrid or other fuel-efficient automobiles, would give a market incentive to move to cleaner forms of energy consumption.

3. The United States should *continue to be a major donor to developing nations through economic aid and direct investment.* Developing countries are currently ill-placed

to address environmental threats caused by industry, in comparison to the greater threat of human poverty caused by joblessness. Commitments to poverty-reduction measures must be made by donor nations, including sustainable development projects such as sustainable farming and irrigation and support of environmentally friendly community projects and businesses.

4. The United States must *return to international negotiations on climate change.* As one of the largest emitters and one of the most influential players, any international environmental agreement suffers without US cooperation. Furthermore, non-cooperation in one area can have repercussions in other areas of international coordination; for example, a downturn in cooperative relations can affect trade partnerships, either directly at the national policy level or at the civil society level via boycotts or simple preferences for the products and services of closer allies.

5. In order to address cataclysmic events such as flooding and hurricanes, which may be attributable to global warming, as well as to contamination of essential resources through pollution or international acts of terrorism, there must be *effective instruments in place for disaster response.* The Federal Emergency Management Agency (FEMA), within the Department of Homeland Security, is currently mandated with this responsibility. Following the outcome of the inquiries related to the response to Hurricane Katrina, the agency must be able to successfully carry out early-warning assessments, rapid deployment to affected areas, and provide a coordinated response with local, state, and other federal bodies. The United States, as the leading world power, should be able to provide effective and near-immediate disaster response to global partners, as well as domestically.

6. *Public awareness and education must be supported though community-level programs and within schools.* Increased public awareness of the negative consequences

of environmental damage will help ensure support for policy makers who support strong measures to counteract such damage. A well-informed civil society that is strengthened by the active support of NGOs and grassroots organizations is the best way to ensure oversight and analysis of government policies.

7. *The Environmental Protection Agency should have the financial means and political independence from the federal administration to conduct independent assessments.* The integrity of the information provided by the agency should be beyond doubt, meaning that employees should not fear censure of their findings and assessments should not be directly funded by parties who have a stake in the results. The agency should be overseen by a non-partisan review board to ensure that these principles are not violated.

Finally, many questions remain on the causes of global climate change and ozone depletion, as well as of the effects of carbon dioxide emissions, water, and air pollution. New methods for farming and irrigation should be explored to prevent food shortages. *The support of scientific research and development*, such as the exploration of alternatives to fossil fuels, is thus essential. A more complete understanding of the root causes of environmental damage and its global impacts can help national governments and international bodies develop the most effective policy responses and facilitate cooperation.

References

[1] The UNDP Human Development Report of 1994 was an early promoter of the concept of human security, which is based on two main pillars in the report: freedom from want and freedom from fear.

[2] According to a *Time* magazine article, "One especially sobering study from the Massachusetts Institute of Technology found that hurricane wind speeds have increased about 50% in the past 50 years. And since warm oceans are such a critical ingredient in hurricane formation, anything that gets the water warming more could get the storms growing worse. Global warming, in theory at least, would be more than sufficient to do that." J. Kluger, "Is Global Warming Fueling Katrina?," *Time*, August 29, 2005.

[3] M. Klare, *Resource Wars: The New Landscape of Global Conflict* (New York: Metropolitan Books, 2001), pp. 138-139. Klare asserts that, in the early decades of the 21st century, wars will be fought over natural commodities to control dwindling supplies.

[4] According to the Carbon Dioxide Information Analysis Center of the US Department of Energy (2002 estimates), the United States has the world's highest net fossil-fuel emissions rate. The per capita emissions rate is 5.52 metric tons of carbon dioxide, ranking the United States eleventh in the world on per capita emissions. Statistics available online: http://cdiac.ornl.gov.

[5] According to David Corn, "As George W. Bush prepared for his recent trip to Europe, he and his advisers continued to dismiss the science underlying the calls for reducing greenhouse gases. The general consensus in the field of climate science, reflected in the work on the Intergovernmental Panel on Climate Change (an international body comprised of hundreds of scientists), is that global temperatures are on the rise—and may climb 10 degrees Fahrenheit this century—and that this increase is, to some degree, a result of human-induced emissions of carbon dioxide and other gases. While there is a small number of contrarian scientists who either argue otherwise or question the basic models, it is undeniable that most experts concur there is a bear in the woods." D. Corn, "George W. Bush: The Un-Science Guy," Alternet, June 19, 2001, available at http://www.alternet.org/story/11054.

[6] Some estimates put the total US membership of environmental groups at over 25 million people, mostly belonging to grassroots organizations. See P. Shabecoff, *A Fierce Green Fire: The American Environmental Movement* (Washington: Island Press, 2003), p. 226.

[7] According to Walter A. Rosenbaum, "business often, if not usually, is able to exploit its privileged status in American politics to ensure that its views are represented early and forcefully at all policy stages, and its forces are mobilized effectively for long periods of time. These are formidable advantages, often enough to give a decisive edge in competitive struggles with environmental or other interests that do not have the political endurance, skill, or resources to be as resolute in bringing pressure on government when it counts." W.A. Rosenbaum, *Environmental Politics and Policy*, 4th ed. (Washington: Congressional Quarterly, Inc., 1998), p. 61.

[8] National Environmental Policy Act of 1969 (Public Law 91-190). Full text available on the website of the Federal Council on Environmental Quality: http://ceq.eh.doe.gov/nepa/regs/nepa/nepaeqia.htm.

[9] D.E. Harmon, *The Environmental Protection Agency* (Philadelphia: Chelsea House Publishers, 2002), p. 36.

[10] United States Department of State, "Fact Sheet: United States Policy on the Kyoto Protocol," available online at http://vienna.usembassy.gov/en/download/pdf/kyoto.pdf.

[11] The United States is seen as reluctant to engage in restrictive, binding international agreements, exemplified not only by its withdrawal from the Kyoto Protocol, but also, for example, by its non-participation in the International Criminal Court. Clear incentives for the United States must be made regarding the benefits of compliance that outweigh the perceived loss of sovereignty that accompanies binding agreements.

[12] National Intelligence Council, "Climate Change and its Implications through 2020," discussion paper presented at the Climate Change Conference, University of Maryland, June 28, 2004.

[13] *Ibid.*

[14] *Ibid.*

[15] Chatham House/National Intelligence Council, "Globalization and Future Architectures: Mapping the Global Future 2020 Project," Conference Report, Chatham House, London, June 6, 2005.

[16] National Intelligence Council, "Mapping the Global Future: Report of the National Intelligence Council's 2020 Project," December 2004, p. 76.

[17] H. Blatt, *America's Environmental Report Card: Are We Making the Grade?* (Cambridge, Mass: Massachusetts Institute of Technology, 2005), p. 233.

CHAPTER 23

EDITORIAL OF POLICY BRIEF ON US ENVIRONMENTAL
POLICY AND GLOBAL SECURITY

NAYEF R.F. AL-RODHAN

Dr. Nayef R.F. Al-Rodhan is Senior Scholar in Geostrategy and Director of the Program on the Geopolitical Implications of Globalization and Transnational Security at the Geneva Centre for Security Policy, Geneva, Switzerland

1. Review and Critique

Environmental security encompasses a gamut of challenges, such as global climate change, water and air pollution, and degradation of scarce resources. As Frank McNeil notes, environmental damage can lead to the increased severity of natural disasters, wreak severe economic harm, cause societal instability, and even contribute to conflicts within nations, as well as across borders.[1] At the most fundamental level, environmental damage and degradation affect human security. Disease caused by water pollution is perhaps one of the most elementary examples of the connection between the environment and human security. Another source of human insecurity linked to environmental damage or degradation is damage to livelihoods.

The challenge of environmental security is often a problem of governance and institutions. At one level, environmental crises are not just linked to environmental degradation and scarcity of resources but also to the lack of, or the inadequate nature of, environmental management policies. As research on the situation in South Asia shows, lack of institutional or governance capacities can often help to account for human insecurity resulting from a lack of scarce resources or the degradation of environmental resources.[2] Environmental degradation does not simply turn into conflict, but it may lead to conflict where there are inadequate means to address the problem.

Yet, environmental security represents a challenge not only at the domestic level but also at the transnational level since the impact of environmental damage or degradation can affect a number of countries. Environmental issues can therefore also become state-level security issues. There have been numerous examples of international conflicts stemming from disputes over transboundary water management, such as in the Nile Basin, the Jordan Basin, the Ganges Basin,[3] and between Mexico and the United States (US).[4]

As Jennifer Wallace points out in her brief, the competing interests of domestic environmental lobbies and industrial business lobbies often provide a major impediment to addressing issues of environmental security. The US case demonstrates this very well. At issue is a conflict between short-term, economic interests and long-term, security interests. Interestingly, the US is not only the largest net contributor of carbon dioxide emissions but is also home to the strongest environmental lobbies.[5] Nevertheless, the US refuses to sign the Kyoto Protocol. The US case is interesting not only from this point of view but also because of its influence on the global agenda.

As Wallace highlights, progress is further complicated by the complexity of identifying the root causes of environmental degradation or damage, which include both natural trends and those induced by man. The scientific evidence linking carbon dioxide and other greenhouse gases to global climate change is also contested. This presents a significant challenge to any agreement on multilateral measures aimed at reducing such emissions.

2. Dilemmas and Our Recommendations

Thus, improving environmental security poses considerable challenges. First and foremost, it poses a challenge to states to develop the necessary institutional and governmental capacities to support environmental management. It also requires prioritization of long-term security interests over short-term economic gains. The US case is pertinent in that it demonstrates some of the obstacles that may be encountered in addressing issues of environmental security. We suggest eight dilemmas or challenges facing US policy makers, as well as eight corresponding recommendations to overcome these challenges.

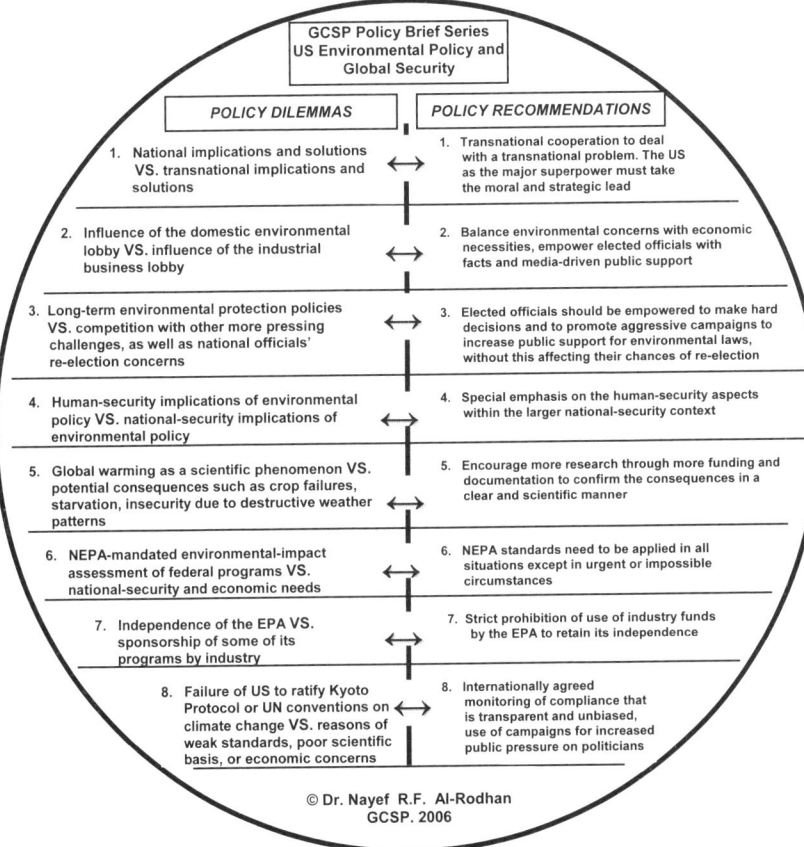

As mentioned, the impact of environmental damage and degradation is felt at both the individual and state level. Thus, policy makers face the challenge of reconciling the human-security with the national-security implications of environmental policy. Doing so requires emphasizing the human-security aspects of environmental security within the larger context of national security. At the same time, it is essential that the transnational implications of environmental damage and degradation form part of policy considerations. It is essential that states engage in transnational cooperation in order to deal with environmental-security questions. Because of US influence, Washington should take the moral and strategic lead on this issue.

One of the factors explaining the lack of US leadership on environmental issues appears to be the conflict of interest between the domestic environmental lobby and the industrial business lobby, and the greater degree of influence exerted by the latter. Ideally, environmental matters should be balanced with economic concerns. This, however, is not the case at present. This is at least partly because the scientific evidence is open to question, leaving policy makers in a relatively weak position from which to promote stricter environmental laws. In order to achieve a better balance between environmental and economic issues, elected officials should be empowered with scientific facts, as well as media-driven, public support. More funding ought to be made available to support further research on global warming. Documentation confirming the consequences of global warming should be provided in a clear and scientific manner.

Policy makers also face the dilemma of whether to focus on long-term environmental-protection policies or seemingly more pressing challenges. A key consideration determining the choices made by elected officials is their re-election. Faced with the possibility of a backlash from special interest groups and the public as the result of potentially unpopular policies, elected officials are likely to avoid making hard decisions from which the benefit will only be felt over the long term. Elected officials should be empowered to make hard decisions and to support aggressive campaigns to increase public support for environmental laws, without affecting their own chances of being re-elected.

Another dilemma is whether to establish environmental-impact assessments of federal programs under the National Environmental Policy Act of 1969 (NEPA). Though it was established some time ago, NEPA still constitutes effective guidelines for federal environmental regulation. In the absence of updated regulatory mechanisms, NEPA standards should be applied in all situations, except in urgent or impossible situations. The independence of the Environmental Protection Agency (EPA) should also be ensured through the strict prohibition of the use of industry funds.

3. Conclusion

Environmental degradation and damage must be considered a security concern. An examination of the US case illustrates some of the difficulties encountered in addressing environmental issues. Reconciling the human- and state-level dimensions of environmental issues requires recognition of the human-security aspects of environmental policies within the broader context of national security. Safeguards also need to be put in place to reduce the influence of the industry business lobby within political and scientific processes.

References

[1] F. McNeil, "Making Sense of Environmental Security," The North-South Agenda Papers, No. 39, Dante B. Fascell North-South Center, University of Miami, 2000, p. 1.

[2] A. Najam, "The Human Dimensions of Environmental Security: Some Insights from South Asia," ECSP Report, Issue No. 9, 2003, available online at http://www.wilsoncenter.org/topics/pubs/ACF23C.pdf.

[3] H. Haftendorn, "Water and International Conflict," paper presented at the 40th Annual Convention of the International Studies Association, Washington, DC, February 16-20, 1999.

[4] A. Peshard-Sverdrup and M. Bishop, "U.S.-Mexico Transboundary Water Management: The Case of the Rio Grande/Rio Bravo: Recommendations for Policymakers for the Medium and Long Term," Center for Strategic and International Studies, January 2003.

[5] For the brief in its entirety, please see Chapter 22.

CHAPTER 24

IDENTIFYING TRANSNATIONAL SOLUTIONS FOR OUR
GLOBALIZED WORLD

NAYEF R.F. AL-RODHAN

Dr. Nayef R.F. Al-Rodhan is Senior Scholar in Geostrategy and Director of the Program on the Geopolitical Implications of Globalization and Transnational Security at the Geneva Centre for Security Policy, Geneva, Switzerland

Conclusion

The way in which states interact in the international system is gradually changing as globalization impacts a number of different processes. This is most apparent in the identification and handling of various transnational threats. This publication has collected a number of policy briefs that focus on the structural aspect of furthering state security and stability, and that discuss how some of the major issues within this debate are currently being handled at the state and regional levels.

Through our assessment of instances of state interaction, such as the Nuclear Non-Proliferation Treaty, arms control, the monitoring, sale, and distribution of natural resources, and the changing role of the North Atlantic Treaty Organisation (NATO), we have outlined some of the major themes for these concluding thoughts.

First of all, it has become clear that globalization has forced states to re-analyze their role and position within the international system. The Westphalian Order no longer applies, neither to states nor to sub-national groups. Nor can the world continue to operate within the structures developed and perfected during the Cold War. The era of globalization and the current workings of multilateral treaties and organizations have forced states to re-examine the norms to which the international system has become accustomed. That means that a new framework must be developed in order to re-define norms and standard operating procedures within international organizations as well as in the traditional system of treaties and agreements. Therefore, the resolution of international problems must also be adapted to modern security demands.

Second, more collective coherence is required at the international level. Currently, national governments will sometimes develop national policies to handle transnational problems and threats. This issue is, in part, addressed in the brief on natural disasters. Most countries have developed national policies for disaster relief, but they are often not comprehensive enough to handle the transnational nature of such disasters. International organizations will therefore play a large role in coordinating relief, but there should be more collaboration between national and international networks in order to empower national governments to handle more of the logistical relief support in the future. Not only will this allow for international logistics to remain where they are needed (for example, in the case of the recent Indian Ocean tsunami, personnel and material were sent from all over the world to assist the relief efforts), but it will also empower national governments to help their own citizenry, which will build confidence and trust in national structures.

Third, implementation of solutions, most notably in the regulation of resources, must be enforced. There are solutions to these problems, and this is certainly also true for environmental policy. While the environmental policy brief focused on the policies of the United States, it should still be noted that the more the major international players cooperate in international environmental policies, the more likely it is that global environmental problems will receive global attention.

Fourth, state institutions must re-evaluate themselves in global terms. This is most notably the case with the changing role of NATO in current international structures. Regional institutions must start to think globally if they wish to remain active and vital parts of the security framework.

There are solutions to the most prominent threats to the international system. Sometimes, finding a solution is the easiest part, while it is often more of a challenge to find the necessary political and economic resources to implement them. States must enact a system of checks and balances within the international framework in order to encourage states to execute current policy recommendations and to facilitate the dialogue and cooperative measures required to meet further systemic demands.

Issues of transnationalism have become the norm. Globalization has allowed national threats to evolve into transnational threats. It is difficult to find problems that exist solely on the national level. Many problems that started as national issues have now reached a transnational stage, thereby making national solutions to such problems obsolete.

Some of the solutions presented to these policy challenges may seem to be fanciful or wishful thinking. However, as the international system works towards transnational solutions to these problems, answers may be found to some of the less formidable security questions. Any progression toward the discovery of further cooperative measures and means to enhance global cohesion will contribute towards a healthier, stronger, and more stable geopolitical system.

INDEX

1994 Agreed Framework, 63
1995 Dayton agreement, 93
1995 NPT Review Conference, 62, 80
2000 NPT Review Conference, 80
2004 Istanbul Summit, 7, 8
2005 NPT Review Conference, 61, 80
2006 International Narcotics Control Strategy Report, 20
9/11, 6, 14, 21

A

Abkhazia, 28
Adi Quala, 136
Afghanistan, 7, 16, 20, 36, 47, 138-139, 150
Africa, 6, 8-9, 40, 170-171, 175,
  sub-Saharan, 109, 170, 180
African Union, 7
AIDS, 170-175, 177, 179-180
Alaska, 112
Algeria, 110
Amu Darya, 131
Angola, 136-137
Annan, Kofi, 61, 77
Antarctica, 40
Anti-personnel landmines, 93
Arab-Israeli War of 1967, 186
Aral Sea, 129
Argentina, 41
Armenia, 29
Arms control, 2, 64, 89-99, 101-104, 203
Arms-control agreements, 61, 64, 95-96

Asbestos Hazard Emergency Responses Act of 1986, 188
Asia, 9, 35, 171, 175
  Asia-Pacific region, 24, 97
  Central Asia, 9, 19, 35, 92, 97, 101, 131
  East Asia, 36, 38, 50-51
  Northeast Asia, 42
  South Asia, 97, 109, 150, 197
  Southeast Asia, 40, 150, 158
Ataturk Dam, 135
Australia, 8-9, 41, 138, 158
  development agency, 152
Avian flu, 27, 171, 176
  see also avian influenza and H5N1 virus
Avian influenza, 175, 179,
  see also avian flu and H5N1 virus
Azerbaijan, 22, 28-29, 31, 36, 107, 110

B

Baghdad, 135, 140
Baiyangdian Lake, 138
Baku-Tbilisi-Ceyhan (BTC) pipeline, 25-26, 110
Balkans, 7, 10
Bangladesh, 136
Belarus, 41, 111
Belgium, 137
Beslan, 22
Bin Abdul Aziz al-Saud, Abdullah, 116
Bin Laden, Osama, 40
Biological weapons, 40, 42, 46, 76-78, 80, 85
Biological Weapons Convention (BWC), 40, 42, 91

Bio-resources, 26, 27
Bio-terrorism, 21
Black Sea, 108
Bosnia and Herzegovina, 136
  Stabilisation Force (SFOR/IFOR), 9
Brazil, 41
Bush, George W., 172
  administration, 20, 99, 187-188
  see also US administration
  President's Emergency Plan for AIDS Relief (PEPFAR), 172, 176

C

Cano Limon oil pipeline, 112
Caribbean, 40
Caspian, 19-21, 23-30
  Basin security force (CASFOR), 22
  Guard program, 22
  Pipeline Consortium, 25
  Sea Maritime Interdiction, 22
  Sea region, 19, 22-24, 26-28, 35-38
  Sea, 19-20, 22-30
  Working Group, 23
  caviar, 21, 26, 37
  fleet, 24
  oil, 29
  policy, 27
  projects, 24
  states, 20-24, 26-29, 31, 35, 38
Caucasus, 8, 19, 35
Cauvery Waters Tribunal, 135
Central Asia Regional Information and Coordination Centre, 22
Chatham House/National Intelligence Council (NIC), 191
Chechnya, 20, 22, 28, 36
Chemical weapons, 42, 50, 76-78, 80, 85
Chemical Weapons Convention (CWC), 40, 42, 80, 91
China National Offshore Oil Company (CNOOC), 115
China, 19-20, 24, 28, 35, 41-42, 51, 55, 69, 80, 83, 101, 108, 110, 114, 120-121, 137-139, 158, 175
  nuclear forces, 39
Chirac, Jacques, 77
Clean Air Act of 1970, 188
Clean Water Act of 1972, 188
Clinton, Bill
  administration, 172
Cold War, 5, 8, 13, 16, 70, 83-84, 89-93, 95, 97-98, 101, 203
  post-Cold War, 94-96, 98
Colombia, 112, 139-140
Colorado River Delta, 129
Commission on Security and Cooperation in Europe (CSCE), 93
Comprehensive Environmental Response, Compensation and Liability Act of 1980 (Superfund), 188
Comprehensive Nuclear Test Ban Treaty (CTBT), 40, 78-79
Convention on International Trade in Endangered Species of Wild Fauna and Flora, 21
Cooperative Threat Reduction (CTR), 63, 94

Cooperative Threat Reduction
(CTR) *continued*
    frameworks, 94
Cuba, 41

D

Danube, 136-137
Darfur, 140
De Hoop Scheffer, Jaap, 7-8
Democratic Republic of Congo,
    136
Dengue fever, 172
Diphtheria, 180
Drug trafficking, 19-22, 27, 30,
    36, 38, 170

E

Earth Liberation Front (ELF),
    139
East Timor, 137
Ebola virus, 172
Economic
    development, 20, 129, 145
    growth, 143, 146, 172
    interests, 23, 198, 185, 187
    security, 36-37, 119, 143, 156,
        164-165, 182, 185-186
Economics, 129, 130-132
Ecuador, 136
ElBaradei, Mohamed, 63, 67,
    84, 86, 102
Energy
    delivery networks, 107, 112
    industry, 107-108, 115, 120-
        121
    infrastructure, 26, 29, 107,
        109, 121
    security, 2, 20, 24-25, 61, 107,
        109-110, 113, 115-116, 119-
        122, 124

Energy *continued*
    supply, 20, 107-110, 112-116,
        119-120, 123
    trade, 107, 109, 113, 116
Energy Policy and Conservation
    Act of 1978,
        188
Environmental Protection
    Agency (EPA), 188, 194,
        199-200
Environmental
    damage, 26, 36, 122, 185-
        187, 189-192, 194, 197-199
    degradation, 13, 19, 36-37, 170,
        185-186, 189, 197-199, 201
    policy, 2, 187, 199, 204
    security, 21, 26, 36, 158, 200,
        187, 197-199
Eritrea, 136
Ethiopia, 136-137, 175
Euphrates, 135, 186
Euro-Atlantic Cooperation
    Council, 7
Europe, 7, 10, 15, 24, 28, 35,
    50, 91, 96, 101, 108, 171,
    175
    Western Europe, 36, 38, 108
European Security and Defence
    Policy (ESDP), 8-9,
        14
European Union (EU), 5-8, 10,
    14-15, 19-20, 24, 28, 35, 43,
    51, 79, 110, 154, 172
    member states, 6, 14-15, 110
EU-US Declaration on
    HIV/AIDS, Malaria and
    Tuberculosis, 172

F

Federal Emergency Management Agency (FEMA), 153, 193
France, 7, 13, 41, 46, 52, 55, 64, 69, 80, 83, 85, 114, 137

G

G8, 6, 63
  Global Partnership, 63, 67, 77
Ganges Basin, 144, 198
Gaza Strip, 140
Georgia, 29, 36, 47
Germany, 110
Global Fund to Fight AIDS, Tuberculosis and Malaria, 172-173, 176
Global Nuclear Energy Partnership (GNEP), 63
Global warming, 108, 111, 155, 165, 186, 191, 193, 199, 200
Gove Dam, 136
Greece, 158
Greenhouse gases, 111, 186, 198
Gulf of Mexico, 109
Gulf War, 135

H

H5N1 virus, 171, 174
  see also avian flu and avian influenza
Health care, 129, 152, 171, 180-182
Health security, 180
Health threats, 169-170, 173-174, 179-182
Highly enriched uranium (HEU), 45-47
HIV, 170-172, 174-175, 177, 179-180

Hong Kong, 171
Human security, 89, 94, 98, 102, 143, 146, 149, 151, 163-165, 171-172, 180, 182, 185-186, 197, 199
Human trafficking, 170
Hurricane Katrina, 149-154, 156, 158, 163, 165, 186, 191, 193
Hurricane Rita, 151
Hussein, Saddam, 39, 45

I

Ice Mountain Water Company, 139
  see also Nestle Waters
India, 19-20, 24, 35, 39, 41, 45-46, 48, 51-52, 55-56, 62-63, 66, 69-71, 80, 83, 97, 101, 110, 114, 120-121, 135, 138-141, 150, 154, 158, 175
  nuclear program, 45
  nuclear status, 46
Indian Ocean, 150, 155, 157
Indian Ocean tsunami, 149-151, 163, 204
Indian Supreme Court, 135
Indonesia, 150, 152, 154-155, 157-158
Inga Dam, 136
Inter-Agency Standing Committee, 154
Intermediate-Range Nuclear Forces (INF), 92
International Atomic Energy Agency (IAEA), 40, 42-43, 45, 47, 50-52, 57-59, 63, 71-72
  inspection rights, 47

International Convention for the Suppression of Acts of Nuclear Terrorism, 79
International Energy Agency (IEA), 108-111, 115, 120
International Organization for Migration (IOM), 154
International security, 2, 5, 14, 39-40, 48, 55-56, 61, 79, 90-91, 95, 129
International Security Assistance Force (ISAF), 9, 15
Iran, 3, 20-23, 31, 35, 37, 39, 42-45, 47-51, 56, 69, 79, 83, 97, 101, 110
  Iranian-US relations, 44
  nuclear facilities, 29, 44, 50
  nuclear program, 20, 28, 43-44, 50
Iraq, 7, 39, 56, 110, 112, 119, 135, 140
  oil production, 109
Islamic Movement of Uzbekistan, 140
Israel, 40-41, 44-45, 50, 52, 55, 62, 66, 69-71, 80, 83, 101, 138
Istanbul Cooperation Initiative (ICI), 6
Istanbul, 135
Italy, 109

J
Japan, 8-9, 42, 51, 110, 114, 158
  government, 110, 172
Joint Oil Data Initiative (JODI), 116, 122
Jordan Basin, 144, 198
Jordan River, 186

K
Kabila, Joseph, 136
Kajaki Dam, 139
Karachi, 138
Kashmir, 139-140, 158
Kazakhstan, 22, 28, 31, 41
Kenya, 138, 141
Khan, A.Q., 45
Khristenko, Viktor, 24-25
Khumbuwan Liberation Front (KLF), 139
Kinshasa, 136
Kosovo, 8, 16, 136-137
  Kosovo Force (KFOR), 9
Kunene River, 136
Kuwait, 135
  Iraq invasion of, 110
  Iraqi occupation of, 109
Kyoto Protocol, 111, 117, 122-123, 188, 198-199

L
Latin America, 40
Lavrov, Sergey, 23
Libya, 45, 47, 63
Liquefied natural gas (LNG), 111
London, 107

M
Macedonia, 139
Malaria, 170, 172, 175, 179
Malaysia, 78
Maldives, 150

Man-Portable Air Defense Systems (MANPADS), 93
Mediterranean Dialogue, 6
Megaports Initiative, 22
Mekong River Commission, 127

Meuse River, 137
Mexico, 140, 144, 198
Middle East, 8-9, 36, 38, 50, 52, 72, 110, 171, 175, 191
Migration, 6, 157, 164, 179
Millennium Development Goals of the United Nations (MDGs), 125-126, 171
Mines other than anti-personnel landmines (MOTAPM), 93
Missile Technology Control Regime, 42
Moscow, 22-23, 25, 43

N
Nagorno-Karabakh, 28, 36
National (state-owned) oil companies (NOCs), 114, 122-123
National Environmental Policy Act of 1969 (NEPA), 188, 199-200
National security, 2, 94, 119, 164-165, 172, 176, 186, 199, 201
Natural gas liquids, 110
Nepal, 139
Nestle Waters, 139
 see also Ice Water Mountain Company
Niger Delta, 112
Nigeria, 119, 175
Nile Basin, 144, 198
Nile Basin Initiative, 127
Nixon, Richard, 188
Non-nuclear-weapons states (NNWS), 50, 64, 66, 69, 78
Non-proliferation regime, 39-41, 47, 49-51, 57-58, 61, 69-72, 75-76, 78-81, 84-85

Non-state actors, 3, 37-38, 39, 46-49, 55-57, 59, 61-62, 64, 70-71, 75-81, 83-86, 91, 94, 101-104, 181
Non-state nuclear suppliers, 81
North Atlantic Treaty Organisation (NATO), 3, 5-10, 13-17, 23, 51, 136-137, 203-204
 member states, 6, 10, 14, 16-17
 Partnership Action Plan Against Terrorism, 6
 Partnership Action Plan on Defense Institution Building, 7
 Response Force (NRF), 9
North Korea, 3, 39, 41-43, 45, 48-51, 56, 63, 69, 83, 97, 101
 missile capabilities, 42
 nuclear ambition, 79
 nuclear capabilities, 42
 nuclear-weapons program, 39
North Sea, 112
Nuclear
 arms, 75-76, 84
 arsenal, 41, 45-46, 52, 57-58, 69, 83, 101
 club, 46, 52, 69
 device, 45-46, 51
 energy, 44, 52, 62-63, 70-72
 enrichment, 50
 facilities, 46, 52, 66
 fuel, 47, 67, 71-72
 industry, 47
 materials, 44, 48, 57-58, 62, 64, 66-67, 70, 75-77, 81, 84, 86, 102
 military programs, 49

Nuclear *continued*
  nuclear proliferation, 40, 57, 69, 72, 75-76, 78
  nuclear non-proliferation, 56, 66, 70, 98
  policy, 44
  power, 112, 114, 191
  power plant, 46, 114
  power program, 43
  program, 55, 58
  technology, 48-49, 57-58, 61, 77-78, 81, 102
  terrorism, 66
  threats, 77
  trafficking, 65
  war, 69
  warhead, 46, 55
  weapons, 41-45, 50-52, 55, 57, 61, 64-66, 69-72, 75-78, 80-81, 83-86, 92, 101, 103-104
  weapons program, 41, 72
  weapons states (NWS), 41, 50, 52, 64, 66, 69, 75, 78, 80, 102-103
Nuclear Non-Proliferation Treaty (NPT), 3, 40-43, 45-52, 55, 57-58, 61-67, 69, 70-72, 78, 80, 83-86, 91, 101-103, 203
Nuclear Suppliers Group (NSG), 63, 67, 71

O
Oil Pollution Act of 1990, 188
Open Skies Treaties, 92
Operation Active Endeavour, 6
Organisation for Economic Co-operation and Development (OECD), 109
Organization for Security and Co-operation in Europe (OSCE), 6, 93
Organization of the Petroleum Exporting Countries (OPEC), 123
Organized crime, 5, 22, 170, 179
Ozirak, 40

P
Pakistan, 7, 39, 41-42, 45-52, 55-56, 62, 66, 69-71, 80, 83, 97, 101, 138, 140-141, 150-156, 158
  earthquake (2005), 149-152, 154, 163
  Federal Relief Commission, 154
Palestine, 138
Paris, 107
Partnership for Peace (PfP), 6-8, 10, 15
Peru, 112, 136
Peruca Dam, 136
PIR Center, 43
Prague and Istanbul Summit documents, 15
Pretoria, 137
Proliferation Security Initiative (PSI), 48, 62, 71, 77, 79, 91
Putin, Vladimir, 27, 40
Pyongyang, 43, 51

R
Radiological weapons, 50
Red Sea, 110
Republic of Korea, 114
  see also South Korea
Resource Conservation and Recovery Act of 1976, 188

Revolutionary Armed Forces of Colombia (FARC), 139
Riga, 8-9
Romania, 41
Russian Federation, 8, 20, 22-25, 27-29, 31, 35, 37-38, 41-43, 46, 50-52, 55, 57, 63, 69, 80, 83, 97, 110, 175, 180

S

Safe Drinking Water Act of 1974, 188
Sarajevo, 136
Saudi Arabia, 50, 110, 116
Second Line of Defense program, 22
Secondary proliferation, 78
Second-tier nuclear proliferation, 78
Severe acute respiratory syndrome (SARS), 171, 174
Shining Path guerrillas, 112
Six-party talks, 39, 63, 79
Societal security, 146
Somalia, 141, 150
South Africa, 41, 137
South Korea, 9, 50, 51
 see also Republic of Korea
South Ossetia, 28
Soviet Union
 see USSR
Sri Lanka, 150, 157-158
START, 92
START-1, 93
START-2, 93
Steinmeier, Frank-Walter, 24
Straits of Hormuz, 109
Strategic North-South Pipeline, 110

Sudan, 7, 9, 140
Sweden, 41
Switzerland, 8, 41
Syr Darya, 131

T

Taiwan, 65
Taliban regime, 7
Tehran, 23, 43-44
Tehran Environmental Convention, 26
Terrorism, 5-6, 13-14, 19-22, 27, 37-38, 98, 119, 131, 135-140, 170, 179, 187, 193
Thailand, 150, 156-157
Toxic Substance Control Act of 1976, 188
TransCaspian Pipeline, 25
Treaty on Arms Trade, 94
Treaty on Conventional Armed Forces in Europe (CFE), 92-93
 Adaptation Agreement to the CFE, 98
Tuberculosis, 170, 172-173, 175, 179-180
Turkey, 19-20, 28, 35, 51, 110, 135, 158, 186
Turkmenistan, 25, 28, 31

U

Ukraine, 28, 41, 109, 111
United Kingdom (UK), 41, 55, 63, 69, 80, 83
United Nations (UN) 6-7, 9-10, 59, 63, 85-86, 103-104, 126, 135-136, 151, 154-155, 158, 165-166, 171, 173, 199

United Nations *continued*
  2006 Report on the Global
    AIDS Epidemic, 175
  Charter, 99
  Disaster Assessment and
    Coordination Team, 154
  Disaster Management Team,
    154
  General Assembly, 79-80
  Framework Convention on
    Climate Change, 111, 188
  Interim Administration
Mission in Kosovo
(UNMOVIK), 62
  International Strategy for
    Disaster Reduction (ISDR),
    150
  Joint Program on HIV/AIDS
    (UNAIDS), 170, 175-176
  Office for the Coordination of
    Humanitarian Affairs
    (OCHA), 152, 154
  Office for the Coordination of
    Humanitarian Affairs
    (OCHA) Tsunami Task
    Force, 154
  Office on Drugs and Crime
    (UNODC), 22
  Security Council, 28, 40, 46,
    48-49, 51-52, 58, 62, 64,
    66-67, 71, 76-77, 79-81
  Special Commission
    (UNSCOM), 62
  Winter Race, Pakistan, 152
United States (US), 6-10, 14, 16,
  19-20, 22-25, 28, 31, 35, 39-44,
  46, 50-52, 55, 57, 59, 63-65,
  68-69, 77-78, 80, 83, 90, 93-
  94, 97, 99, 107-110, 114,

United States *continued*
  120, 125, 132, 134-135, 139-
  140, 144, 149-150, 152-154,
  158, 163, 172, 185-188, 190,
  192-193, 197-201, 204
  administration, 43, 77, 90
  see also Bush administration
  Central Command, 22
  Central Intelligence Agency
    (CIA), 172
  Congress, 63, 115
  Department of Defense, 22
  Department of Homeland
    Security, 193
  environmental discourse, 187
  environmental policy, 185,
    197, 199
  European Command, 22-23
  global agenda, 7
  government, 97, 187-188,
    190, 192
  Iranian-US relations, 44
  leadership, 90, 192, 200
  National Intelligence Council,
    175
  National Intelligence Estimate,
    172
  national security, 172
  Peace Corps, 154
  Pentagon, 41
  policy, 25, 44
  policy agenda, 189
  Senate, 153
  Special Forces, 51
  State Department, 20, 25
  State Department Country
    Reports on Terrorism, 21
  US-European relations, 9
  US-India nuclear agreement,
    46

Unocal Corporation, 115
USSR, 19, 25, 35, 41, 55, 69, 77, 83, 93

V
Vienna Document on Confidence- and Security-Building Measures, 92

W
Washington, DC, 16, 44, 97, 200
Washington Treaty, 6
Water Conflict Chronology, 126, 131, 135
Weapons of mass destruction (WMD), 2, 5, 6, 19-22, 27, 36, 38-40, 42, 46, 48-50, 52, 55-57, 59, 63, 84, 101
  policies, 56
West Nile virus, 172
World Bank, 127, 170, 174
World Commission on Dams, 133
World Health Organization (WHO), 152, 173, 176-177, 180
World War II, 92

Y
Yellow River, 129
Yugoslavia, 136-137

Z
Zambia, 136